ASHKELON DISCOVERED

*From Canaanites and Philistines to
Romans and Moslems*

Ashkelon Discovered

From Canaanites and Philistines to Romans and Moslems

By Lawrence E. Stager

Director, Leon Levy Expedition to Ashkelon

With a contribution by Paula Wapnish

BIBLICAL ARCHAEOLOGY SOCIETY
WASHINGTON, DC

Library of Congress Catalog Card Number: 91-073339
ISBN 0-9613089-8-2

© 1991

Biblical Archaeology Society
3000 Connecticut Avenue, NW
Washington, DC 20008

Reprinted from *Biblical Archaeology Review*
March/April 1991
May/June 1991
July/August 1991

This book
is dedicated to
Shelby White and Leon Levy,
true connoisseurs and
patrons of the arts.

Ashkelon Discovered—
From Canaanites and Philistines
To Romans and Moslems

About the Authors   **viii**

Foreword   **1**
HERSHEL SHANKS

I. When Canaanites and Philistines Ruled Ashkelon   **2**

II. Why Were Hundreds of Dogs Buried at Ashkelon?   **20**

III. Eroticism and Infanticide at Ashkelon   **38**

Beauty and Utility in Bone—   **58**
New Light on Bone Crafting
PAULA WAPNISH

Readers Vote to Print Erotic Oil Lamps   **63**
Letters to the Editor

About the Authors

Lawrence E. Stager is Dorot Professor of the archaeology of Israel at Harvard University, director of the Harvard Semitic Museum and director of the Leon Levy Expedition to Ashkelon. Author of many articles based on his field work in Carthage, Cyprus and in the Judean Desert, he is a trustee of the American Schools of Oriental Research and former vice-president of the Archaeological Institute of America.

Stager's previous articles in *Biblical Archaeology Review* include "Child Sacrifice at Carthage—Religious Rite or Population Control?" (co-authored with Samuel R. Wolff, **BAR**, Jan./Feb. 1984) and "The Song of Deborah—Why Some Tribes Answered the Call and Others Did Not" (**BAR**, Jan./Feb. 1989) for which he won the Fellner Award for the best **BAR** article of 1989.

Paula Wapnish teaches history at the University of Alabama at Birmingham and has worked at Ashkelon and Tell Jemmeh in Israel and in Turkey, Lebanon and Iran. Co-author of *Animal Bone Archaeology: From Objectives to Analysis* (with Brian Hesse, Taraxacum, 1985), she studies animal bones in order to identify changing patterns of diet and animal exploitation from the Late Bronze period through the Iron Ages.

Foreword

When I asked Larry Stager to write an article for *Biblical Archaeology Review* on his excavations at Ashkelon—and he agreed—neither of us had any idea how things would turn out.

A couple of months before his manuscript was due, the silver calf was uncovered—a discovery that made the front page of the *New York Times* and brought a horde of journalists to his doorstep. For the moment, all scientific work stopped.

Then, too, Larry does not write easily. This is because every thought is carefully crafted before it goes on paper. And this says nothing about the exhaustive research that precedes the writing.

Not surprisingly, Larry missed his initial deadline. So we decided that he would submit his manuscript in segments so as to feed it as quickly as possible into our editorial process and production mill.

When the first segment arrived, I immediately realized that it would make a wonderful article by itself. If we added the balance of the text—yet to come—we would have to delete many of the pictures. The answer was obvious, especially as we had all kinds of deadlines staring us in the face: Print the article in two parts in successive issues.

That is what we decided to do. Then we concentrated on polishing the first segment and preparing it for the printer. The result was that we were late with the second segment. You know the result. The second segment itself came in segments, the first of which was itself a wonderful article. So we announced that instead of a two-part article, it would be a three-part article.

As soon as the third and final segment went to press, we realized that all three parts should be bound together in a book. The whole is a moving account of an excavation that will be studied and cited a hundred years from now, an excavation that is bringing to light new aspects of civilizations of which we are all the inheritors—both for better and for worse.

It seemed only natural to add to this publication Paula Wapnish's insightful article on bone manufacturing. Paula's new and original research is based almost wholly on artifacts excavated at Ashkelon.

Finally, we have added the results of our readers' poll on whether we should print pictures of the erotic lamps uncovered in a Roman-period villa. Deciding whether to print these sexually explicit pictures was difficult. On the one hand, we are a scientific, objective journal that reports on life in ancient times; and these lamps, found in an excavation we were reporting about, were definitely part of that life. On the other hand, many of our readers would be offended by these pictures, especially because **BAR** is often read by youngsters, both in Sunday schools and otherwise. After considerable agonizing, we decided to let our readers make the decision. The result, as reported on p. 63, is that 20 percent voted against printing the pictures, 50 percent voted for printing them, and 30 percent voted to print them with a perforation so they could be cut out by those who felt they were inappropriate in the magazine. In short, 80 percent of our readers said, in one way or another, print them. We think they made a wise decision. Readers of this book may wish to see the views of our readers on this delicate—or indelicate—subject, so we also included some of their letters here.

It is with great pride that the *Biblical Archaeology Review* brings all these materials together within the same covers.

None of this would have happened—from the first spade in the ground to the eventual final report that will some day be published on this continuing excavation—without the interest and generous support of Leon Levy and his wife Shelby White. To them, we are all deeply grateful.

Hershel Shanks
Editor
Biblical Archaeology Review

June 1991

LISTINES RULED ASHKELON

PHOTOS BY CARL ANDREWS

Ashkelon. The summer of 1990. The sixth season of the Leon Levy Expedition, sponsored by the Harvard Semitic Museum. In the waning days of the season, on the outskirts of the Canaanite city, we excavated an exquisitely crafted statuette of a silver calf, a religious icon associated with the worship of El or Baal in Canaan and, later, with the Israelite God, Yahweh. The calf lay buried in the debris on the ancient rampart that had protected the city in the Middle Bronze Age (c. 2000-1550 B.C.).

The calf was housed in a pottery vessel in the shape of a miniature religious shrine, which itself had been placed in one of the storerooms of a sanctuary on the slope shortly before the destruction of the seaport in about 1550 B.C. The date is secure. Other pottery found in the sanctuary dates to the terminal phase of the Middle Bronze Age (MB IIC, c. 1600-1550 B.C.).

A merchant approaching the Canaanite city from the Mediterranean on the road leading up from the sea would have been dwarfed by the imposing earthworks and towering fortifications on the northern slope of the

Preceding pages: *A daunting slope outside Ashkelon's northern gate would have dissuaded many an attacker bent on conquest. At bottom center (where the people are clustered) are the excavated rooms of the sanctuary of the silver calf (inset).*

The approximately 40-degree slope is not a natural feature but rather an artificial earthwork that was the base of an enormous fortification system throughout much of Ashkelon's history. The ramparts date to Middle Bronze II (2000-1550 B.C.) and were rebuilt four times in that period alone. The earliest layer of the slope was capped with mudbricks. The later three were capped with rows of rough field stones; tamped earth or mud plaster, about 4 inches thick, covered the stones and gave the slope a smooth exterior surface.

The drawing at right shows the slope's major defensive features: A mudbrick tower, now badly deteriorated, of the Middle Bronze IIC period (1600-1550 B.C.) is at upper left. Another massive mudbrick tower, at upper right, was built by the Philistines in Iron Age I (1200-1000 B.C.). In front of the Philistine tower lie thick layers of artificial fills that formed the slope, or glacis, of the Philistine rampart. Rising behind it are remnants of Hellenistic fortifications, made of medium-sized ashlar blocks of sandstone.

The artist's rendition (below), with its exaggerated, "fisheye" angles, depicts how Ashkelon's northern gate might have appeared in the 16th century B.C. A visitor, perhaps a seafaring trader from Phoenicia, might well have paused at the Sanctuary of the Calf at the base of the slope (center) to present an offering of thanks for a safe journey and then made his way up the slope to the impressive twin-towered gate. The sanctuary was not directly below the gate but below and to the right of it—perhaps because the path up the slope was at an angle rather than head-on to the gate, thus making the climb easier.

Abutting the Mediterranean Sea in modern-day Israel, Ashkelon was a center, in turn, of Canaanite, Philistine, Phoenician, Roman, Byzantine and Islamic cultures. It was a member of the Philistine pentapolis, or league of five cities, and appears frequently in the Bible. Samson killed 30 men there in a rage (Judges 14:19); David, after he heard of the deaths of Saul and Jonathan, cried, "Publish it not in the streets of Ashkelon" (2 Samuel 1:20); and Zephaniah predicted that "Ashkelon shall become a desolation" (Zephaniah 2:4).

The excavations here are casting new light on Canaanite and early Israelite religious practices and are helping solve one of the most controversial issues in Biblical archaeology: When did the Philistines arrive on the shores of Canaan?

city. About 300 feet along his ascent from the sea, he might have paused to make an offering at the Sanctuary of the Silver Calf, just off the roadway to the right—nestled in the lower flank of the rampart. Farther up the road to the east, the merchant would have entered the vast metropolis of Ashkelon through the city gate on the north.

The silver calf was nearly complete and assembled when we found it. Only one horn was missing, and only the right foreleg was detached from the rest of the body. Less than 4.5 inches long and 4 inches high, the calf nevertheless weighs nearly a pound (14 oz.). It is a superb example of Canaanite metalwork. The delicate and naturalistic rendering of the features leave no doubt about the quality of the craftsmanship—or about the age and sex of the small animal: It is a young male calf, yet old enough to have developed horns. The body is made of bronze; only 2 to 5 percent is tin, the rest, copper. It was cast solid, except for the horns, ears and tail and the right foreleg and left hindleg. These two legs were cast separately and joined to the rest of the calf by tenons (projections) and riveted in place. The sole surviving horn, the ears and the tail were made of forged copper*

---

* Forged copper is heated, hammered and cooled until the desired shape is attained.

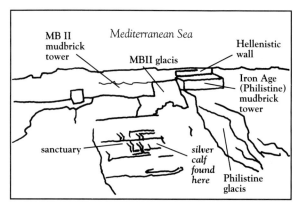

RICHARD CLEAVE

Ashkelon on the sea. *An arc of earthworks one-and-a-half miles long encloses the immense 150-acre ancient city. Built over a 3,500-year span, from 2000 B.C. to 1500 A.D., the protective rampart defines the flat, semicircular mound on which the ancient city stood. Today the Yadin National Park, named after famed Israeli archaeologist Yigael Yadin, who died in 1984, lies inside the 150-acre mound.*

and inserted into the body. Tenons also extended below the hooves. These were obviously used to mount the statuette on a small platform or dais, which perished or disappeared in antiquity. The calf was once completely covered with a thick overleaf of pure silver. Deep grooves running along the back and underside of its bronze body and around its neck still contain remnants of the silver sheet. Some of the silver overleaf has also survived on the legs, head and tail.

The ceramic model shrine that housed the calf is a cylinder with a beehive roof. It has a knob on top of the roof and a flat bottom. A doorway raised slightly above the floor is just large enough for the calf to pass through. Hinge scars on the door jambs indicate where a separate clay door had once been fitted into place.

The silver calf was just one of the many splendors of Ashkelon during this period, the apex of Canaanite culture in the Levant. During the first half of the second millennium B.C., Askhelon was one of the largest and richest seaports in the Mediterranean. Its massive ramparts formed an arc of earthworks extending over a mile and a half and enclosing a city of more than 150 acres, with probably 15,000 inhabitants,

nestled beside the sea. On the north side of the city, where we excavated, the gates and fortifications had been rebuilt at least four times during the 150 years of the Middle Bronze IIB-C periods (1700-1550 B.C.).

This magnificent city was probably destroyed by the Egyptians in the aftermath of the "Hyksos expulsion." The Hyksos were an Asiatic people, probably Canaanites (some of whom might have originated in Ashkelon),

who had imposed Canaanite hegemony over much of Egypt during the Second Intermediate Period (c. 1650-1550 B.C.), until the Egyptians managed to expel them forcibly, pursuing them back into Canaan.

The silver calf from Ashkelon is a very early, rare example of bovine iconography in metal. Bull or calf symbolism expressed in metal and other media was associated with El or Baal, leading deities in the Canaanite pantheon. This tradition provided the progenitors of later Biblical iconography that linked Yahweh, the Israelite God, with golden and silver calf-images.

During their formative period (before about 1200 B.C.), the early Israelites borrowed heavily from Canaanite culture, even while, at the same time, they distanced themselves from their neighbors. When, in about 925 B.C. the kingdom split in two, with Israel in the north and Judah in the south, Jeroboam, the first king of the northern kingdom installed "golden calves" in the official sanctuaries at Dan and Bethel. The association of Yahweh with such images was obviously acceptable there. However, prophets like Hosea and rival priests from Jerusalem (the capital of the southern kingdom) condemned calf symbolism as idolatry. The words of Hosea not only provide us with a polemic against calf iconography, they also tell us how these images were made and how they were revered:

> "Ephraim [the northern kingdom] was . . . guilty of Baal-worship; he suffered death. Yet now they sin more and more; they cast for themselves images; they use their silver to make idols, all fashioned by craftsmen. It is said of Ephraim: 'They offer human sacrifices and kiss calf-images'" (Hosea 13:1-2, Revised English Bible).

With but this taste of Canaanite Ashkelon, let us pass on to Philistine Ashkelon. That is the Ashkelon of the Bible.

Both Biblical and cuneiform texts make it clear that Ashkelon was a Philistine city during most of the Iron Age (c. 1200-586 B.C.). During that time it was a member of the famous Philistine Pentapolis* that also

* See Trude Dothan and Seymour Gitin, "Ekron of the Philistines, Part I" and "Ekron, Part II," **BAR**, January/February and March/April 1990, respectively.

First glance. *Shelby White, writer and connoisseur of ancient Near Eastern art, points to a metal calf minutes after its discovery within a sanctuary at the base of Ashkelon's north slope. The diminutive figurine (4.5 inches long and 4 inches high) electrified the excavators and became the highlight of the 1990 dig season. Lying shattered in pieces around the calf are remnants of the pottery shrine that housed the calf. The sanctuary was destroyed, together with much of the city, probably by the Egyptians in about 1550 B.C.*

The calf, cast of solid bronze, was found remarkably well preserved; only the right foreleg had become detached from the rest of the body and the left horn was missing. The right foreleg and left hindleg were cast separately and riveted into the body. The remaining horn, the ears and the tail were of forged copper and were also inserted into the body. Grooves along the calf's back and underside and around the neck still contain silver, as do parts of the legs, head and tail, leading excavators to conclude that the figurine was once completely covered by a sheet of silver.

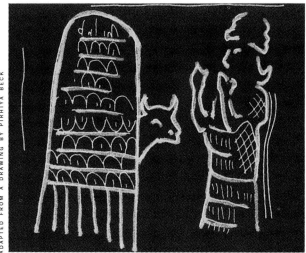

included Ekron, Gaza, Gath and Ashdod. When the Philistines (or an earlier vanguard of their ethnic tradition) arrived in coastal Canaan is a hotly debated issue, to which we will return later.

In 604 B.C. Ashkelon, like its sister-city Ekron, was destroyed by King Nebuchadrezzar (also called Nebuchadnezzar) and his neo-Babylonian army. Less than 20 years later (in 586 B.C.) Nebuchadrezzar would destroy Jerusalem and the Temple built by King Solomon.

The last Philistine king of Ashkelon, Aga', and his sons, as well as sailors and various nobles, were exiled to Babylon, just as many Jews were after the fall of Jerusalem. Unlike the Jews, however, we hear nothing about the return of the Philistines to their native land. Those that remained behind later lost their ethnic identity, although the region they once occupied and dominated culturally, was still identified as Philistia, or Palestine, by the Romans hundreds of years later; today, many Arabs call themselves Palestinians, echoing their Philistine namesakes of the distant past.

When my predecessor at Ashkelon, the British archaeologist John Garstang, readied his expedition in 1920, he supposed that Philistine Ashkelon was a comparatively small site, occupying only the south mound known as al-Hadra, a mere 15 acres. He had no idea that, even there, the Philistine cities lay buried under 12 to 15 feet of later civilizations. Digging from the top of the mound, Garstang soon despaired of ever reaching anything earlier than the Hellenistic period. After two seasons of excavation (1920-1921), he abandoned Ashkelon for a less complicated site.

During that same two-season period, however, Garstang's young assistant, W. Phythian-Adams was rather more clever. He succeeded in locating both earlier Philistine and Canaanite levels.

Phythian-Adams nibbled away at the north (Grid 38) and west (between Grids 50 and 57) sides of al-Hadra with two step trenches. These small-scale excavations documented a continuous sequence of occupation from about 2000 B.C. (beginning of Middle Bronze IIA) to the modern era. Unfortunately, Phythian-Adams recorded the location of these two step trenches, one no bigger than a telephone booth, only by the designation of the plot number on the official Ottoman land registry. These numbers identify fields approximately 300 feet long. Nevertheless, it was our very good fortune to have established our two main trenches next to his during our opening season. Once we discovered this, we were reassured that here Iron and Bronze Age levels lay below later cultural remains.

What we did not know, until last season, was how big Philistine Ashkelon really was. Over 2,000 feet north of al-Hadra, we found Philistine fortifications—a massive mudbrick tower 34 feet by 20 feet and a huge glacis-type* rampart. These protected a Philistine seaport not of 15 acres, but of over 150 acres. These fortifications were built in about 1150 B.C. Ashkelon, like Ekron and Ashdod (also recently excavated), was a large, heavily fortified city of the Philistines. Farther north at Dor, a city of the Sikils (according to the Egyptian "Tale of Wen-Amon"), excavations have revealed not only the Sea Peoples' harbor but also their fortifications and glacis of the 12th century B.C.[1]

* See Neil Silberman, Glossary, "A Question of Defense: Glacis, Casemate Wall and Offset-Inset Wall," **BAR**, May/June 1989.

Its shrine repaired, the Ashkelon silver calf (photo, right) stands beneath the proud gaze of author Stager, Ashkelon's chief excavator. The last people to have viewed the calf and shrine as they now appear were Canaanite worshippers living nearly 3,600 years ago.

The opening of the shrine is just wide enough for the calf to pass through. A clay door once covered the opening. The excavators believe the calf was displayed emerging from the shrine, much like the calf or bull depicted in the drawing at left. The image, engraved on a second-millennium B.C. cylinder seal from Acemhöyük, in Anatolia (modern-day Turkey), shows the animal poking its head from its shrine and a suppliant with raised hands.

The Hebrew Bible is filled with invective against calf worship, most famously in the incident of the Golden Calf (Exodus 32). The prophet Hosea said derisively of the northern kingdom of Israel: "They offer human sacrifices and kiss calf-images" (Hosea 13:2). The Canaanites associated calf or bull images with the worship of El or Baal, the most important deities in their pantheon of gods. Many scholars believe the Israelites emerged from Canaanite society a little before 1200 B.C.; scholars conjecture that the Israelites' abhorrence of calf worship stems from their need to distance themselves from Canaanite religious practice.

The Massive Middle Bronze Fortifications—
How Did They Work?

Numerous theories have attempted to explain the function of the immense sloping defensive structures that enclosed many ancient cities in the Middle Bronze Age II (2000-1550 B.C.). Why so wide at the base? The rampart at Ashkelon, for example, is more than 50 feet high and more than 75 feet at the base.

At one time, most scholars attributed these formidable MB II fortifications to the "Hyksos," the enigmatic and supposedly non-Semitic people from the north, who, with their superior weapons of war, invaded and conquered Canaan and Egypt in the 17th century B.C. The Hyksos had chariots, even at this early date. Ashkelon's excavator, British archaeologist John Garstang, believed that Ashkelon's earthworks, like those of the "Lower City" of Hazor, surrounded, not a city, but a huge chariot park. Storing chariots and their horses required a wide, protected area; hence the huge earthworks. The inhabited portion of Ashkelon, Garstang thought, was confined to a small mound inside the wide arc of the earthen embankments.

Other scholars proposed that the earthworks were related to chariotry, but for the opposite purpose: to keep them out rather than in.

Yigael Yadin dispelled both notions. His excavations at Hazor showed that the city extended throughout the lower portions of the site and was surrounded by impressive earthworks that formed the base of the fortification system. The earthworks, in other words, surrounded not a chariot park but an entire city. We now believe this to be true at Ashkelon as well. As for the other theory—that the earthworks were meant to repel chariots—Yadin pointed out that chariot warfare took place not around cities but in open plains away from cities.

Yadin believed the earthworks at Hazor were built to counter the battering ram, also once thought to have been introduced by the Hyksos. This seems highly unlikely, however, since we know that in later periods, the besiegers, such as the Assyrian king Sennacherib at Lachish* in 701 B.C. and the Romans at Masada in 73 A.D., actually *built* sloping siege ramps in order to move their battering rams into position for attacking weak points in the fortification line, such as the city gate. So I doubt that these huge earthworks were intended to counter the use of battering rams; they might have even aided in their use.

Archaeologists Peter Parr and G. R. H. Wright have proposed a more banal function for the sloping ramparts: to counter erosion of the tell, or artificial hill, formed by superimposed layers of settlement. The tell of some cities reached a considerable artificial height by the second millennium B.C. But surely, there must have been more energy-efficient and less costly ways of countering erosion than by installing tons and tons of earthen embankments around the site.

I would like to propose another solution. I agree with Yadin that the MB II ramparts were a defense against siege warfare. But these thick sloping embankments, often surrounded by a ditch or dry moat, were designed, not to counter battering rams; rather they were built in response to another very ancient city-conquering technique—tunneling, mining and sapping—in common use even in the medieval period, in fact right up to the invention of gunpowder.

While the city was under siege, a team of excavators from the attacking army would begin their tunnel at some distance from the fortification line they wished to undermine. Their object was to cause the fortifications to collapse or to sneak beneath them and then to surface inside the city, usually at night, to launch a surprise attack. It might take days, even weeks, for the "moles" to reach their objective. Once under the fortifications they might widen the tunnel in order to collapse the defenseworks above, or if that failed, to stoke the widened tunnel with combustibles, which would then be burned in order to precipitate collapse, while

---

* See David Ussishkin, "Answers at Lachish," BAR, November/December 1979; Hershel Shanks, "Destruction of Judean Fortress Portrayed In Dramatic Eighth-Century B.C. Pictures," BAR, March/April 1984; and David Ussishkin, "Defensive Judean Counter-Ramp Found At Lachish in 1983 Season," BAR, March/April 1984.

---

assault troops penetrated the breach above ground.

Obviously, the thick earthen ramparts of Ashkelon and many other Canaanite cities posed a serious obstacle to this siege technique. The amount of debris the tunnelers would have had to remove before reaching the wall line and towers was so great that this would give scouting parties, sent out by the besieged city, adequate time to spot the sappers and trap them or smoke them out. The ditch which surrounded many such ramparts was, whenever possible, dug to bedrock. This prevented the sappers from beginning their tunnel beyond the ditch and would give the scouts of the besieged city a better chance at spotting the entrance to a tunnel.

Tunneling through an MB II rampart was not only slow but also quite dangerous: The sand and soil fills, such as were used at Ashkelon, would have been extremely unstable. The tunnels would have been extremely susceptible to collapse (we know from experience just how unstable the balks or standing sections are at Ashkelon after more than one collapse).

When I presented this hypothesis to the premier military historian of the ancient Near East, Professor Israel Ephal of the Hebrew University, he was quick to accept the idea and then informed me that there was even an Akkadian word, *pilšu*, that describes just such a siege technique, and it was already in common use by the early second millennium B.C. Thus the sapping or tunneling technique was known and used precisely at the time we find massive fortifications appearing in Syria and Canaan.

My conclusion is that the construction of immense sloping structures at the base of the city wall was not introduced by the Hyksos as foreign invaders. Indeed, the "Hyksos" were really Canaanites, anyway, as we now know from Manfred Bietak's excavations at Tell-ed-Dab`a, the Hyksos capital of Avaris in the Egyptian Delta. This fortification technique was an indigenous innovation of Canaanite cities to counter the besiegers' tactic of tunneling to undermine the battlements or to enter the city clandestinely.-L.E.S.

In contrast to the Israelites, especially the rustic ridge-dwellers of the central hill country, the Philistines of the plain appear to have been far more urbane and sophisticated, thus belying the dictionary definition of a Philistine as a person who is lacking in or smugly indifferent to culture and aesthetic refinement. This negative portrayal derives ultimately from the Bible, of course, written by bitter enemies of the Philistines. When the early Israelites were using coarse, unpainted pottery, for example, the Philistines were already decorating their pottery with imaginative bichrome motifs and figures, such as fishes and birds.

Our staff zoo-archaeologists, Dr. Paula Wapnish and Professor Brian Hesse of the University of Alabama in Birmingham, have begun to document a rather dramatic shift in domesticated species at the end of the Late Bronze Age (13th century B.C.) and the beginning of the Iron Age (12th century B.C.). The shift is from sheep and goats to pigs and cattle. This shift occurred at Ashkelon and other coastal sites, but not in the central highland villages of the same period dominated by Israelites—settlements like Ai, Raddana and Ebal.[2] From a strictly ecological perspective, this seems surprising. The oak-pine-and-terebinth woodlands that dominated the central hill country of Canaan, where the earliest Israelite settlements of about 1200 B.C. are

to be found, are ideally suited for pig production, especially because of the shade and acorns. One reason why such a hog-acorn economy did not thrive in the early Israelite environment must ultimately be rooted in very early religious taboos that forbade the consumption of pork. If so, these findings would nullify the hypothesis of anthropologist Marvin Harris that "kosher" rules can be explained primarily by ecological considerations.[3] These findings would also contradict those scholars who argue for a much later date for the introduction of these dietary restrictions.

As noted earlier, when the Philistines arrived on the coast of Canaan is still a vexed question, although it is becoming increasingly clear where they came from. Two leading experts in the definition of Philistine culture, Professors Trude and Moshe Dothan, have argued that a generation before the Philistines themselves arrived, a pre-Philistine group of Sea Peoples landed on the coast of Canaan. The arrival of the Philistines is marked, in their view, by the appearance in Canaan of what has become known as Philistine bichrome ware, a distinctive red and black decorated pottery. An earlier monochrome pottery has been identified by them with an

(text continues on p. 13)

ILAN SZTULMAN

The Canaanite way of death. *An adolescent Canaanite girl lies in a flexed position in a mudbrick-lined vault covered with wooden boughs and coated with white plaster (left), dating to about 1500 B.C. At her shoulder the excavators found two toggle pins, for fastening a garment; three Egyptian scarabs and an ivory roundel lay on her midsection.*

The photo above shows the other items found in the burial: a Red-Polished Syrian flask (center, rear); two Base-Ring juglets (right) imported from Cyprus, which may have contained opium; and two bowls, seen as found in the photo at left, one with a food offering of a lamb or goat chop and a small bird (perhaps a dove or a partridge).

The scarabs and the Cypriot pottery imports helped excavators date the burial to about 1500 B.C., indicating that Ashkelon had revived after the Egyptians destroyed parts of the seaport about 50 years earlier. The custom of burying within the city, rather than in a cemetery outside it, and the mudbrick-lined vault are continuations of Middle Bronze II (2000-1550 B.C.) Canaanite burial traditions.

CARL ANDREWS

When Did the Philistines Arrive in Canaan?
Multiple Clues Help Unravel the Mystery

The question of when the Philistines arrived in Canaan—and more generally when the Sea Peoples (of which the Philistines were one) arrived in the Levant—and just where they came from is finally being answered.

One key is an Egyptian wall relief (opposite, top) on the temple of Karnak, in Thebes. Long thought to have been commissioned by Pharaoh Ramesses II (1279-1212 B.C.), the relief has recently been shown to depict a series of campaigns conducted in Canaan in 1207 B.C. by Merenptah (1212-1202 B.C.), son of Ramesses II.* The scene shown here is of the siege of Ashkelon, identified as such by the hieroglyphics at top center. The desperate inhabitants beg for mercy while the battle rages below them. An oversize pharaoh dominates the right portion of the scene. What is crucial in this scene is that the inhabitants are depicted with the same dress as undoubted Canaanites in other, adjacent reliefs—and without the distinctive headgear and clothing with which the Philistines and other Sea Peoples are depicted in other Egyptian reliefs. The Philistines, we must therefore conclude, had not yet arrived in Canaan in 1207 B.C.

When they did arrive is shown by a second Egyptian wall relief, at Medinet Habu (shown in reconstruction opposite, bottom). The relief dates to about 1175 B.C., during the reign of Ramesses III (1182-1151 B.C.), and depicts a naval battle between Egyptian ships (left) and those of the Sea Peoples, including the Philistines (center and right), called Peleset in the hieroglyphics that accompany the relief. The Sea Peoples can be identified by their distinctive headgear, which consist of feathered headdresses.

* Frank J. Yurco, "3,200-Year-Old Picture of Israelites Found in Egypt," **BAR**, September/October 1990.

JAMES WHITRED

TERRY SMITH

MONOCHROME POTTERY

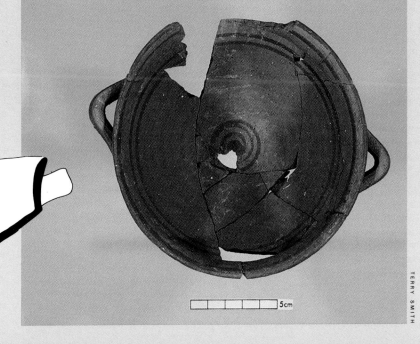

DR. ABBAS ALIZADEH

TERRY SMITH

5cm

JAMES WHITRED

At about the same time the battle recorded at Medinet Habu was taking place, a new type of pottery was making its appearance in Canaan. Known as Mycenaean IIIC1, or monochrome, pottery, it is Mycenaean in style but made of local clays. In Canaan, examples have been uncovered at Ashdod and Ekron, and now at Ashkelon. The photo on the preceding page (top) shows a portion of floor beneath a public building with columns that contained monochrome pottery. As the name implies, monochrome pottery is decorated with only a single color (black or red), such as in the sherds at center of the preceding page and on the inside of the carinated bowl (preceding page, bottom), all dating to about 1175-1150 B.C. The profile drawing shows the carination, or the sharply angled body, of the bowl; the left half of the drawing shows the outside of the bowl, while the right half is a cutaway view showing the bowl's thickness. The most commonly found decorations on the outside of Philistine monochrome pottery are antithetic spirals (that is, mirror-image spirals set next to each other—as in the center photo) and horizontal bands; less common were net-patterned lozenges and wing motifs; on the interiors, they feature horizontal bands and spirals.

One level higher in the floor, dating to the latter half of the 12th century B.C., were examples of the next stage of

BICHROME POTTERY ▲ ▼

JAMES WHITRED

pottery evolution, called Philistine bichrome. These are decorated in two colors, red and black, as in the pictures above. The top photo shows a bichrome bell-shaped bowl with wing motif uncovered in 1920-21 by the British archaeologists John Garstang and W. Phythian-Adams. Bichrome pottery frequently features antithetic spirals, red and black checkerboard patterns, birds and, rarely, fish.

Author Stager notes that after about 1175 B.C. the locally made monochrome pottery in Canaan began to diverge in style from the monochrome pottery that was being manufactured in the Aegean. Coupled with the evidence provided by the two Egyptian wall reliefs discussed above, Stager concludes that the Philistines were Aegean peoples—specifically Mycenaean Greeks—who came to Canaan *en masse* in about 1175 B.C.

(continued from p. 9)

earlier generation of pre-Philistine Sea Peoples.[4]

Unlike the Dothans, I believe this earlier monochrome pottery indicates the earliest phase of Philistine settlement in southern Canaan, just as it serves as the hallmark of new groups of Sea Peoples settling all along the Levantine coast and in Cyprus in the first half of the 12th century B.C. Trude Dothan has provided us with a detailed typology of the hybrid pottery style known as Philistine bichrome ware. Her analysis leaves little doubt that this distinctive red and black decorated pottery, as well as many of its shapes and motifs, derives ultimately from the Mycenaean Greek world, with more limited inspiration from Cypriot, Egyptian and Canaanite sources. However, recent excavations at three of the five members of the Philistine Pentapolis—Ashdod, Ekron (Tel Miqne) and now Ashkelon—indicate the direct antecedent of this bichrome ware was a monochrome pottery even closer to Mycenaean Greek pottery prototypes than the bichrome ware.[5] Moreover, the monochrome pottery was made in Canaan, as we know from the clays.

At Ashkelon in Grid 38 (lower) we have documented stratigraphically the sequence from monochrome ware (Mycenaean IIIC:1) to bichrome ware (Philistine). Beneath the floors of a large public building with thick stone column drums was an earlier building. On its floor lay the earliest Philistine pottery yet discovered at Ashkelon; carinated bowls with strap handles and bell-shaped bowls, decorated with monochrome antithetic spirals, horizontal bands, net-patterned lozenges and tongue and wing motifs on the exterior and with horizontal bands and spirals on the interior.

When did the Philistines arrive en masse on the shores of Canaan? An early contingent of Sea Peoples fought with the Libyans against the Egyptian pharaoh Merneptah (1212-1202 B.C.), as we know from the famous Merneptah Stele, but the Peleset, or Philistines, were not among them. Merneptah quelled another revolt in 1207 B.C., also recorded on the Merneptah Stele, led by the Canaanites of Ashkelon, Gezer, Yanoam and the Israelites. That there were Canaanites, rather than Sea Peoples, in Ashkelon at this time is shown by wall reliefs once assigned to Ramesses II—now properly dated to his son Merneptah—apparently depicting his Canaanite campaign.* The people inside the ramparts of Ashkelon are depicted in these reliefs as Canaanites, not as Sea Peoples. Moreover, at that time Mycenaean and Cypriot pottery was still being imported into the Levant. So the Sea Peoples apparently did not arrive in Canaan until after the reign of Merneptah.[6]

Not until the reign of Ramesses III (1182-1151 B.C.) do we find the locally made Mycenaean-style pottery in the Levant diverging from the earlier and purer Mycenaean prototypes. This reflects a change from trade items coming from comparatively few production centers in the Mediterranean world to locally manufactured pottery at a number of regional centers.

In his famous inscription known as the "War Against the Sea Peoples," Ramesses III describes the Philistine approach to Canaan and his subsequent victory over them. He refers to the Philistines by their name as written in Egyptian hieroglyphics, "Peleset." In accompanying reliefs on the walls of the temple at Medinet Habu, Ramesses III depicts the Philistines, as well as other well-armed Sea Peoples. These reliefs date to about 1175 B.C. These Philistines should be identified with the monochrome pottery that appears in Canaan at about this time.

In short, although Philistine bichrome ware was once thought to herald the arrival of the Philistines early in the reign of Ramesses III (c. 1180-1175), it now appears that the bichrome pottery was dated a bit too early. The monochrome pottery that appears a generation earlier actually marks the first appearance of the Philistines in Canaan, during the reign of Ramesses III.[7]

A closer look at this pottery will also help solve the riddle of Philistine origins.

When tested by neutron activation analysis,** the early monochrome Mycenaean IIIC pottery proved to have been made from local clays, whether at Ashdod and Ekron in Philistia or at Enkomi, Kition and Old Paphos on Cyprus.[8] Almost none of it was imported. Although we must always be cautious about inferring new peoples from pots, I think it can be argued in this case that when this locally made Mycenaean pottery appears in quantity in the eastern Mediterranean, it indeed marks the arrival of the Sea Peoples. Their path of destruction along the eastern Mediterranean coast can be traced from Cilicia, in southwest Turkey, at such sites as Miletus and Tarsus, to the Amuq (or Plains of Antioch), south to Ibn Hani (the seaside resort of the kings of Ugarit in the 14th and 13th centuries B.C.), in Syria; farther south to coastal Canaan at Acco; and on down the coast through Philistia.[9]

As these groups of peoples migrated throughout the eastern Mediterranean coast, their potters no longer shared a common tradition. Thus, it makes little sense to try to put the Mycenaean IIIC styles into an interregional sequence, since local styles quickly diverged from a common template, influenced as they were by very different local surroundings.[10]

When the Philistines first arrived in southern Canaan (c. 1175 B.C.), they made Mycenaean-style pottery using the local clays. Later, in about 1150 B.C., they assimilated Canaanite, Egyptian and other motifs, making the hybrid that archaeologists have for years called "Philistine" pottery. Perhaps we should now call it second-generation Philistine pottery. In fact, the Philistines arrived on the coast and settled in the Pentapolis a generation or more before the production of the bichrome pottery that bears their name.

What we have outlined archaeologically and dated

* See Frank J. Yurco, "3,200-Year-Old Picture of Israelites Found in Egypt," **BAR**, September/October 1990.

** Neutron activation analysis can detect some of the rarest elements present in pottery. By comparing the chemical "fingerprint" of the potsherd to that of various clay sources, it is often possible to determine the provenance of pottery. See Maureen F. Kaplan, "Using Neutron Activation Analysis to Establish the Provenance of Pottery," **BAR**, March 1976.

JAMES WHITRED

to the early part of Pharaoh Ramesses III's reign is described in very vivid terms by Ramesses III himself in his "War Against the Sea Peoples":

"Dateline: Year 8 under the Majesty of Ramesses III [c. 1175 B.C.]: . . . The foreign countries [Sea Peoples] made a conspiracy in their islands. All at once the lands were removed and scattered in the fray. No land could stand before their arms, from Hatti, Kode [Cilicia], Carchemish, Arzawa and Alashiya [Cyprus] on, being cut off at [one time]. A camp [was set up] in one place in Amor [Amurru]. They desolated its people, and its land was like that which has never come into being. They were coming forward toward Egypt, while the flame was prepared before them. Their confederation [of Sea Peoples] was the Philistines, Tjeker [=Sikils], Shekelesh, Denye(n) and Weshesh lands united."[11]

As a logical inference from the archaeological evidence, we may add the following: If the makers of the local monochrome Mycenaean pottery (IIIC:1) settling along the coast from Cilicia in Anatolia to Cyprus and Israel are not Mycenaean Greeks themselves, then we must conclude that they studied their potmaking in Mycenaean workshops. And then they somehow convinced all of their "barbarian" consumers that this pottery was what they should use. Throwing caution to the wind, I am willing to reject these possibilities and state flatly that the Sea Peoples, including the Philistines, were Mycenaean Greeks.

I am willing to speculate even further: When we do discover Philistine texts at Ashkelon or elsewhere in Philistia (and it's only a matter of time until this happens), those texts will be in Mycenaean Greek (that is, in Linear B or some related script). At that moment, we will be able to recover another lost civilization for world history.

We partially excavated two public buildings that were used in both the monochrome and bichrome phases of the Philistine occupation of Ashkelon. These two public buildings produced more than 150 enigmatic artifacts—thick cylinders of unbaked clay, slightly pinched at the waist. More than one row of these cylinders were found lying on the floors of both buildings. Whatever the function of these cylinders, it appears that the same type of activity was carried on in both the monochrome and bichrome phases of these 12th-century B.C. buildings.

As we were excavating these strange cylinders at Ashkelon, at nearby Tel Miqne (which the excavators identify as the Philistine city of Ekron) the diggers were finding the same strange objects at their site. Could they be tablets prepared for inscribing? Would we be able to find the first real evidence of Philistine writing? At both Ashkelon and Miqne, the dig directors eagerly tried to find the first signs of Philistine writings on these unbaked "tablets." But, alas, not a trace was found!

We then shifted to a more banal reading of the evidence. The alignment of the clay cylinders next to walls suggested that they had been dropped from vertical looms. Yet they looked unlike any loomweights we had ever seen. They were unperforated; Levantine loomweights had holes through which the vertical strand of thread from the loom was attached.

Egon Lass, research associate and grid supervisor, finally solved the mystery. His job includes systematically collecting samples from every square yard of excavated floors or surfaces at Ashkelon, and then wet-sieving them. In this way, Lass discovered that occupational debris from the floors with the strange, lined-up clay cylinders contained concentrations of fibers, fibers that could not be detected with the naked eye during excavation, but that appeared only after wet-sieving. Since these cylinders were associated with the weaving industry, they probably were loomweights. The thread was tied around the pinched waist, which was why they were not perforated with holes.

This homely clue looms (forgive the pun) large for determining the cultural homeland of the Philistines and other Sea Peoples.

To the pottery evidence, we can now add the even more persuasive evidence of the lowly loomweights found in abundance at both Ashkelon and Miqne-Ekron. Surely

Humble, yet telling in *their implications, 150 cylinders of unbaked clay (below) lay on the floors of two 12th-century B.C. buildings (photo at left).*

Excavators of the Philistine city of Ekron (Tel Miqne) also found small cylindrical objects very similar to those at Ashkelon. Thinking that perhaps they were clay writing tablets of some kind, both teams of excavators were hoping to find the first-ever examples of Philistine writing on these cylinders, but soon had to settle for a more mundane explanation of the objects' function: Tiny remnants of fibers, not visible to the human eye but found in the dirt nearby, indicated that the small clay objects were loomweights used in weaving. Their shape—pinched at the waist and not perforated—argues for a Mycenaean Greek origin for the Philistines: While perforated loomweights were common elsewhere, unperforated weights such as those at Ashkelon and Ekron have been discovered in Cyprus at Kition and Enkomi (both known to have been settled by the Sea Peoples of Mycenaean Greek origin) and indeed even in Mycenae itself.

these artifacts made of unbaked clay, yet quite different from the local Levantine perforated type, were not imported from abroad, but were made and used by immigrant weavers.

In this same period (early 12th century B.C.), Achaeans or Mycenaeans are thought to have arrived *en masse* on Cyprus (Alashiya).* At two of the Cypriot settlements, Kition and Enkomi, this same type of unperforated loomweight (or "reels" as the excavators there called them) were found in abundance (along with the perforated Levantine ones) in rooms where weaving was being done. The most striking evidence for the origin of the Philistines and other Sea Peoples, however, is the appearance of cylindrical unperforated loomweights in the Mycenaean homeland itself, at centers such as Tiryns, Pylos and Mycenae. When the great archaeological pioneer Heinrich Schliemann was digging at Mycenae, he found numerous cylinders of unbaked clay, but was puzzled about what they were used for. By the time he finished work at Tiryns, where they were also quite common, he rightly surmised that "apparently they were used as weights for looms."[12] In this as in so many other instances, we have learned to take Schliemann's hunches seriously.

Another clue to the Greek connection is the name of one of the Sea Peoples mentioned in Ramesses III's inscription, the Denyen, who have often been equated with the Danaoi of Homeric tradition. The latter term, frequent in the *Iliad*, is used interchangeably in Homer with "Achaeans," who were, of course, the Greeks.

Despite this Greek connection with Danaoi and the archaeological evidence of Philistines in Canaan, scholars have been hesitant to identify all the Sea Peoples with the Mycenaean Greeks. The Greeks are usually considered a minor constituent of the "barbarian" hordes that comprised the Sea Peoples. Modern connotations of "Philistine" (inspired, no doubt, by Biblical pejoratives) have not put scholars in a frame of mind

* See translation of Ramesses III inscription, on p. 14, in which Alashiya is one of the countries overwhelmed by the Sea Peoples.

JAMES WHITRED

A Mediterranean wanderer. *Found in the excavations at Ashkelon, this terra-cotta mold (left) and an impression made from it (right) depict Odysseus (also known by his Latinized name, Ulysses), the hero of Homer's Odyssey, battling the sea monster Scylla. Dating to the Roman period (first-second centuries A.D.), the impression shows Odysseus' spear pointing to the right. The sea monster's tail whips in front of Odysseus' face; heads of oarsmen can be seen below the spear and the head of the helmsman can be seen above the spear butt. The Odyssey describes the scene: "I put on my glorious armor and, taking up two long spears in my hands, I stood bestriding the vessel's foredeck at the prow, for I expected Scylla of the rocks to appear first from that direction."*

The Odyssey is the tale of Odysseus' ten-year-long trek home from the Trojan War. Greek mythology is filled with tales of heroes wandering the eastern Mediterranean world after the war. Stager observes that these tales, as well as the founding myths of many Near Eastern cities (which claim to have been founded by figures from Aegean lands) contain more than a kernel of truth: He believes, for example, that the land of Canaan was settled by Mycenaean Greeks in the 12th century B.C. As this terra-cotta mold shows, the tale of Odysseus' wandering was known in Ashkelon as late as the first or second centuries A.D.

that allows easy acceptance of these Sea People "barbarians" as elevated Greeks. But that is what the archaeology suggests. Nor has our upbringing in the classics helped; indeed it has probably hindered us from recognizing that the heroes of the *Iliad* and the *Odyssey*—the "good guys"—just might be akin to the "bad guys"—namely, the Sea Peoples.

According to Greek epic traditions, which give us the same story from the Greek perspective, some time after the Trojan War (the most widely accepted traditional date for the fall of Troy is about 1183 B.C.), several heroes were celebrated as shipwrecked wanderers trying desperately to return home to mainland Greece. The classic homecoming story is the *Odyssey*. Before Menelaus (who started the whole thing when he married Helen of Troy) returned to his native Sparta after the war, he wandered to Cyprus, Phoenicia, Egypt and Libya. During these difficult, but lucrative, wanderings, Menelaus accumulated much wealth, including such sumptuous items as "two silver bathtubs, and a pair of tripods, and ten talents of gold"—all given to him as "gifts" (however reluctantly) by an Egyptian from Thebes (*Odyssey* IV, 128-129).[13]

Odysseus himself, the hero of the *Odyssey*, got into trouble in Egypt, when Zeus "put it into [Odysseus'] head to go with roving pirates to Egypt." Odysseus' roguish companions plundered the fields of the Egyptians, captured women and children and killed the men. But the Egyptians did not sit idly by; they mounted a counterattack. According to the Odyssey, many of the Greek pirates were killed; others were led into captivity and made to work at forced labor. Luckily, Odysseus (for some unstated reason) was sent to Cyprus (*Odyssey* XVII, 425-445).

The adventures of Odysseus were still celebrated in Ashkelon in the Roman period, as I realized after piec-

ing together what little remained of a pottery mold for making plaques. The mold depicted a warrior with spear and shield in hand standing before the mast. Below him were oarsmen and, to his right, a steersman. The key to the scene, however, is the tail of some kind of sea monster that whips up beside the defending warrior. The scene on the mold recalls the hair-raising episode of Odysseus and the six-headed sea monster Scylla (or Skylla) described in the *Odyssey* (Book XII, 80ff.). Shortly before six of his men were devoured by Scylla, Odysseus ordered his crew to "Sit well, all of you, to your oarlocks, and dash your oars deep into the breaking surf of the water, so in that way Zeus might grant that we get clear of this danger and flee away from it. For you, steersman, I have this order; so store it deeply in your mind, as you control the steering oar of this hollow ship. . . ." The visual imprint of Homer's words lay before us in this terra-cotta mold, with oarsmen and steersman clearly depicted but in Roman style of the first or second century A.D. The story was apparently celebrated in Ashkelon by people who still recalled their Greek heritage hundreds of years later.

Greek legends preserve many "homecoming" stories. In one of these epics (the fragmentary *Nostoi*[14]) some of the Greek heroes never make it back home after the Trojan War. Instead, they wander about the eastern Mediterranean, often with large followings of refugees, founding cities as they go. These founding legends have been preserved at local shrines dedicated to the founding hero.

Among the more remarkable founding stories dealing with what the German scholar Fritz Schachermeyr called the "Achaean Diaspora" are accounts of the colonization of Pamphylia and Cilicia in Asia Minor and Phoenicia on the coast of Canaan—from Colophon in the north to Ashkelon in the south.[15]

According to later legends, many Greeks left Troy for parts south under the leadership of one seer named Amphilochus and another named Calchas. At Clarus near Colophon, one Mopsus, who would become the

recently Trude Dothan and Seymour Gitin have found a sequence of circular, sunken stone-lined hearths in a monumental building at Philistine Miqne,* apparently another Greek element introduced into Canaan by the Philistines, or Sea Peoples.

This archaeological and textual analysis has led me to the inescapable conclusion that two very different cultures and peoples—one Semitic (comprised of Canaanites and Israelites); the other Greek—lived side by side in parts of Canaan.

In the context of these sometimes hostile, sometimes friendly neighbors, we are better able to understand some Biblical heroes as well as villains.

From this perspective it is not so fanciful to imagine Goliath (1 Samuel 17), the Philistine champion whom young David slew with his slingshot, as a mighty, well-armed warrior, similar to Achaeans like Achilles and Odysseus. At the very least, Goliath was equipped much more like an Achaean warrior, complete with bronze greaves on his legs, than like a Canaanite or Israelite soldier (for whom greaves were totally alien).

The adventures of the mighty Samson also reflect a Greek connection. Although the Bible identifies him as an Israelite hero from the tribe of Dan, he does not fit the mold of a typical Biblical Judge of the period, nor is he a leader of Israelite armies like the other Judges. He is instead an individual champion about whom many a tale was told. As recognized by many 19th-century Biblical scholars, Samson is much more like a Greek hero—specifically like Herakles—than a Biblical Judge.[20] In an insightful phrase in *Paradise Lost*, John Milton refers to our hero as the "Herculean Samson."

Samson is the only riddle-teller in the Bible. At his wedding feast to an unnamed Philistine woman from Timnah, Samson propounded this rather bad riddle to the 30 young men at the feast:

> "Out of the eater came something to eat,
> Out of the strong came something sweet."
> Judges 14:14

To know the answer to the riddle you must know that a year earlier Samson had killed a lion with his bare hands. When he passed by the spot on his way to his wedding, he found that a swarm of bees had made their home in the lion's carcass. He scooped out the honey and ate it with his hands.

The guests of course did not know this, so they could not guess the answer to the riddle. After much cajoling, however, Samson finally tells his Philistine bride the answer, which she promptly reveals on the last day of the feast to the male guests. And they answered:

> "What is sweeter than honey,
> And what is stronger than a lion?

Samson then responded (with a trace of barnyard humor):

> "Had you not plowed with my heifer
> You would not have guessed my riddle!"
> Judges 14:18

founding hero of Ashkelon, defeated Calchas in a riddle contest. Tradition has preserved several different riddles that led to Calchas' defeat; here is one of them:

> "[Another] question propounded by Calchas was in regard to a pregnant sow, how many pigs she carried, and Mopsus said, 'Three, one of which is a female' . . . . When Mopsus proved to have spoken the truth, Calchas died of grief."[16]

Riddles were very serious business indeed! Having replaced the original seer Calchas, Mopsus went on to lead his people across the Taurus Mountains into Pamphylia, where he founded two important cities: Aspendus and Phaselis. Mopsus then led other Achaeans on through Cilicia, founding Mallus and Mopsuestia (Mopsus' hearth). From Cilicia, Mopsus marched down the coast all the way to Ashkelon, where, according to the fifth-century Lydian historian Xanthus, Mopsus threw the statue of the mermaid goddess Atargatis (=Tanit/Ashtarte/Asherah) into her own sacred lake. Mopsus, according to this tradition, died in Ashkelon.[17]

According to Richard Barnett, Mopsus is the "first figure of Greek mythology to emerge into historical reality."[18] He says this because a bilingual inscription from the eighth century B.C., written in hieroglyphic Luwian and in Phoenician, was found at Karatepe in Cilicia. In this inscription, Azatiwatas, servant of the king of the Danuniyim (Homer's Danaoi), traces his lineage through the "house of MPŠ (=Mopsus)," indicating that there may have been a kernel of truth behind these Greek founding legends. I mentioned above that one of the cities Mopsus founded was Mopsuestia, which means Mopsus' hearth. Hearths were well known in Aegean and Anatolian cultures, but not in Canaan. Recently however, Israeli archaeologist Amihai Mazar discovered a small raised hearth in a public building adjacent to a Philistine temple at Tel Qasile.[19] Even more

* See photo, **BAR**, January/February 1990, p. 35.

Unlike the Greek seer Calchas, who died of grief when his riddle was answered, Samson simply pays off his bet of 30 linen tunics and 30 sets of clothing by going down to Philistine Ashkelon and killing 30 of its men. He strips them and gives their wardrobes to the guests who had answered the riddle.

Samson is also famous for his seven magical locks of hair. The Biblical writers transformed Samson into a Nazarite, a man dedicated to God. But, although he does not cut his hair, Samson hardly qualifies as the usual Nazarite: He drinks strong drink whenever he likes. Samson's long locks endow him with superhuman strength, however. When shorn, he is, the Bible says, much weaker, "like any man" (Judges 16:17). There is a parallel in Greek epic: Scylla cut her father's hair while he slept, thus removing his invincibility. The king was then captured by King Minos.[21]

The riddle, the magic locks and a hero of superhuman strength were not the stuff of Canaanite or Hebrew lore; they were, however, very much a part of the later Greek, and probably Mycenaean-Minoan, world.

The adventures of Samson took place in the foothills of Canaan, the Shephelah, an intermediate zone of economic, social and cultural exchange between Greeks and Israelites, between Philistines and Hebrews. This border zone with its hybrid cultural elements is reflected not only in the stories we have examined but in the archaeology as well. It is significant, I think, that archaeologists using material culture data have always been confused about the ethnic and cultural affinities of the inhabitants of this intermediate zone during Iron Age I (1200-1000 B.C.). Was Beth Shemesh, on the edge of the Shephelah, for example, an Israelite or a Philistine settlement during stratum III, the Iron I stratum? The signals are confusing and disagreement abounds.

The ancient inhabitants were probably no less confused, for this was taboo territory, the meeting-ground of alien cultures.

Indeed, there is some uncertainty and confusion about the very identity of Samson's tribe, Dan. Were the Danites originally Israelites or did they trace their origins to the Danaoi, the Greeks of Homeric epic?

According to Yigael Yadin, Cyrus H. Gordon and Allen H. Jones, the Danites of the Bible were identical with the Homeric Danaoi, the Egyptian Denyen (in Ramesses III's inscription), the Danuna (in the Amarna Letters of the 14th century B.C.) and the *DNNYM* (in a Phoenician inscription from Karatepe).[22] According to Yadin's reading of the Biblical text, Dan "dwells on ships" (Judges 5:17). Unlike other Israelite tribes, Dan lacks a genealogy (Genesis 46:23; cf. Numbers 26:42). Yadin therefore concludes that Dan was not one of the original Israelite tribes in the early confederation; nevertheless, "Dan shall judge his people as one of the tribes of Israel" (Genesis 49:16). Yadin went even further and attempted to locate the Denyen/Danaoi/Danites in the area around Tel Aviv in the 12th century B.C., where he specifically identified the earliest settlement at Tel Qasile, stratum XII, with these immigrants. Eventually the Danites migrated north and established themselves at Laish/Dan in the north (Judges 18), by which time they were thoroughly integrated into the Tribal League of Israel during the period of the Judges.

While at first glance this hypothesis is extremely appealing, there are many reasons for rejecting it upon further reflection. First and foremost, texts relating to the Sea Peoples give us no indication about the location of the Denyen in the Levant. In the Amarna letters the Danuna seem to be somewhere north of Ugarit in modern Syria. By the time of the Egyptian "Tale of Wen-Amon" (about 1050 B.C.), the Tjeker (or Sikils), occupied the seaport of Dor and surrounding territories.[23] Slightly earlier, the Onomasticon of Amenope (about 1100 B.C.) lists Philistines (Peleset), Sikils and Sherden—all Sea Peoples—living on the coast of the Levant. If this list is in geographical order, then the Philistines represent southern Canaan; the Sikils, the Dor region; and the Sherden, the Acco area.[24] In none of these texts are the Denyen even mentioned; however, this might be expected if in fact they migrated to Laish/Dan before 1100 B.C., as Avraham Biram, the excavator of Laish/Dan, believes they did. Unfortunately, for the Danite=Danaoi hypothesis, the earliest settlement at Laish/Dan which could plausibly be linked to the Danites (stratum VI) has yielded very little Philistine pottery; rather it is characterized by collared-rim store jars and pits—artifacts and features commonly associated with the early Israelites.[25] Furthermore, the Biblical texts relating to the Danites are open to other interpretations. The key text for Yadin—"And Dan, why did he remain in ships?" (Judges 5:17)—can also be interpreted to mean those Danites who served as clients on the ships of the Phoenicians or even the Sea Peoples.* In other words, the Danites were in a client/patron relationship with one of the seafaring peoples of the Levant, but this does not imply that the Danites themselves were Sea Peoples, or Phoenicians. As the Samson story indicates, the Danites were an Israelite tribe located on the western periphery of early Israel even before they moved north to Laish/Dan but were probably under the heavy influence of their coastal Sea Peoples neighbors.

The Samson saga represents a literary genre that Harvard Professor Frank Cross has labeled a "border epic" where two very different cultures—early Greek and Israelite—met on the coast of Canaan. The historical milieu, as I have reconstructed it first from archaeology and then assisted by texts, is a dynamic one in which these two very different cultures encounter each other, interact and transform their respective traditions. 𝕊

* See Lawrence E. Stager, "The Song of Deborah—Why Some Tribes Answered the Call and Others Did Not," **BAR,** January/February 1989.

Photos courtesy Leon Levy Expedition.

[1] Personal communication from Ephraim Stern, Professor of Archaeology, Institute of Archaeology, Hebrew University.

[2] See Brian Hesse, "Animal Use at Tel Miqne–Ekron in the Bronze Age and Iron Age," *Bulletin of the American Schools of Oriental Research* (*BASOR*) 264 (1986), pp. 17-27; also his report on the 1985 faunal remains from Ashkelon in *Ashkelon I*, forthcoming, Harvard Semitic Museum Archaeology and Ancient History series (Cambridge, MA: Harvard Univ. Press).

[3] Marvin Harris, *Cows, Pigs, Wars and Witches: The Riddles of Culture* (New York: Random House/Vintage, 1975), pp. 35-57.

[4] Trude Dothan, *The Philistines and Their Material Culture* (New Haven, CT: Yale Univ. Press, 1982); for their most recent statement, see Trude Dothan, "The Arrival of the Sea Peoples: Cultural Diversity in Early Iron Age Canaan," pp. 1-22, and Moshe Dothan, "Archaeological Evidence for Movements of the Early 'Sea Peoples' in Canaan," pp. 59-70, both in *Recent Excavations in Israel: Studies in Iron Age Archaeology*, ed. Seymour Gitin and William G. Dever, Annual of the American Schools of Oriental Research 49 (Winona Lake, IN: Eisenbrauns, 1989).

[5] We need not imagine, as some scholars once did, that non-Mycenaean motifs of Philistine bichrome ware were acquired during the peregrinations of the Philistines around the eastern Mediterranean (e.g., Cyprus and Egypt) before landing in Canaan. All of these sources of inspiration were right at hand in Canaan itself. Even bichrome decoration itself was known in Phoenicia during the 13th century B.C. and has been found at Ashkelon (this LB IIB bichrome should not be confused with the earlier LB I bichrome, which originated in Cyprus).

In her most recent assessment, Trude Dothan ("The Arrival of the Sea Peoples") has made a fine typological distinction between the Mycenaean IIIC:1 decoration, which she characterizes as Simple Style, and the Philistine bichrome decoration, which she associates with the Elaborate Style known in other parts of the eastern Mediterranean. With this distinction she implies in a more subtle way than before two "waves" of Sea Peoples: The pre-Philistine group makes and uses Simple Style; they are then either augmented or replaced by the later group, the Philistines, who produce Elaborate Style pottery.

It would be an extraordinary development, indeed, if a pre-Philistine group of Sea Peoples preceded in establishing new and impressive cities and then were displaced at each of the Pentapolis sites by the Philistines a decade or two later. It seems much more likely that the relatively minor developments in style from monochrome simple to bichrome elaborate represent changes within the potting tradition of the same people and culture as the second generation of Philistine potters assimilate some of the local Canaanite and other traditions. In other words, Philistine bichrome pottery represents a regional style that developed in south Canaan. It seems likely that other immigrant groups of Sea Peoples settling in the northern coastal Levant, in Cyprus and in the central Mediterranean—for example, Sardinia, Sicily and Italy—might develop distinctive regional styles as they come in contact with different indigenous cultures.

[6] Lawrence E. Stager, "Merenptah, Israel and Sea Peoples: New Light on an Old Relief," *Eretz-Israel* 18 (1985), pp. 61-62.

[7] See Stager, "Merenptah, Israel and Sea Peoples." Using other lines of reasoning, both Amihai Mazar ("The Emergence of the Philistine Material Culture," *Israel Exploration Journal* 35 [1985], pp. 95-107) and Itamar Singer ("The Beginning of Philistine Settlement in Canaan and the Northern Boundary of Philistia" *Tel Aviv* 12 [1985], pp. 109-122) reached similar conclusions.

[8] F. Asaro, Isadore Perlman and Moshe Dothan, "An Introductory Study of Mycenaean IIIC:1 Ware from Tel Ashod," *Archaeometry* 13 (1971), pp. 169-175; Asaro and Perlman, "Provenience Studies of Mycenaean Pottery Employing Neutron Activation Analysis," in *The Mycenaeans in the Eastern Mediterranean, Acts of the International Archaeological Symposium* (Nicosia, Cyprus: Department of Antiquities, 1973), pp. 213-224; Jan Gunneweg, Trude Dothan, Perlman and Seymour Gitin, "On the Origin of Pottery from Tel Miqne-Ekron," *BASOR* 264 (1986), pp. 3-16.

[9] See Stager, "Merenptah, Israel and Sea Peoples," p. 64, n. 37 for bibliography of sites through 1985. To this list we should add Dothan, 1989, (see endnote 5).

[10] See endnote 5.

[11] John A. Wilson, transl. in *Ancient Near Eastern Texts* (*ANET*), ed. James B. Pritchard (Princeton: Princeton Univ. Press, 1969), p. 262.

[12] Heinrich Schliemann, *Tiryns: The Prehistoric Palace of the Kings of Tiryns* (New York: Scribner's, 1885), pp. 146-147. For Kition, see Vassos Karageorghis and M. Demas, *Excavations at Kition: The Pre-Phoenician Levels*, vol. V: Part 1 (Nicosia: Cyprus Dept. of Antiquities, 1985), for example, pl. 20:1087; pl. 34:1020, 1024; pl. 57:1024; pl. 117:5150-5156; pl. 195:5149-5156.

[13] All references to Homer's *Odyssey* follow the translation of Richard Lattimore, *The Odyssey of Homer* (New York: Harper & Row, 1965).

[14] Stubbings, "The Recession of Mycenaean Civilization," *Cambridge Ancient History*, (*CAH*), eds. I.E.S. Edwards, C.J. Gadd, N.G.L. Hammond and E. Sollberger (Cambridge, UK: Cambridge Univ. Press, 3rd edition 1975), vol. II, part 2: *History of the Middle East and the Aegean Region c. 1380-1000 B.C.*, pp. 354-358.

[15] Fritz Schachermeyr, *Griechische Frühgeschichte: ein Versuch, frühe Geschichte wenigstens in Umrissen verständlich zu machen* (Vienna: Osterreichischen Akademie der Wissenschaften, 1984), pp. 181-190.

[16] Strabo, *The Geography*, XIV, 1.27.

[17] Schachermeyr, *Griechische Frühgeschichte*, pp. 183-185.

[18] Richard D. Barnett, "The Sea Peoples," *CAH*, vol. II. part 2, pp. 363-365, and "Phrygia and the Peoples of Anatolia in the Iron Age," *CAH*, vol. II, part 2, pp. 441-442.

[19] Amihai Mazar, *Excavations at Tell Qasile: Part One, The Philistine Sanctuary: Architecture and Cult Objects*, Qedem 12 (Jerusalem: Hebrew Univ. Press, 1980).

[20] See citations and discussion in George Foote Moore, *A Critical and Exegetical Commentary on Judges* (International Critical Commentary) (New York: Scribner's, 1895), pp. 364-365.

[21] Othniel Margalith, "Samson's Riddle and Samson's Magic Locks," *Vetus Testamentum* (*VT*), 36 (1986), pp. 225-234.

[22] Yigael Yadin, "'And Dan, why did he remain in ships?'" *Australian Journal of Biblical Archaeology* 1 (1968), pp. 9-23; Cyrus Gordon, "The Mediterranean Factor in the Old Testament," *VT*, Suppl. 9 (1962), pp. 19-31; Allen H. Jones, *Bronze Age Civilization: The Philistines and the Danites* (Public Affairs Press: Washington, D.C., 1975); Hershel Shanks, "Danaans and Danites—Were the Hebrew Greek?" **BAR**, June 1976.

[23] See John A. Wilson, *ANET*, p. 28, for Wen-Amon, where Dor is called a "town of the Tjeker (=Sikil)." Recently Dr. Avner Raban, of the Center for Maritime Studies at Haifa University, has discovered the remains of the ancient harbor used by Wen-Amon in the 11th century B.C. at Dor (see Raban, "The Harbor of the Sea Peoples at Dor," *Biblical Archaeologist* 50 [1987], pp. 118-126.) The terrestrial archaeologist at Dor, Professor Ephraim Stern, considers the fortification system with glacis to have been built initially by the Sea Peoples, and specifically by the Sikils (personal communication). Shortly before the fall of Ugarit at the hands of the Sea Peoples, the Šikalayū, "who live on ships," were raiding and kidnapping along the coast, according to one Akkadian letter found at Ugarit (RS 34.129). Among the last tablets written there the last king of Ugarit despairs, saying: "The enemy ships are already here, they have set fire to my towns and have done very great damage in the country" (RS 20.238). These seafarers and pirates (the Šikalayū = "Sikils") later moved down the coast and settled in the region of Dor.

Several scholars misidentified the Šikalayū with the Sea Peoples group known as Shekelesh (e.g., G.A. Lehmann, "Die Šikalayū—ein neues Zeugnis zu den 'Seevölker'—Heerfahrten im späten 13 Jh. V. Chr. [RS 34. 129]," *Ugarit Forschung* 11 [1979], pp. 481-494).

Anson Rainey was the first scholar to identify correctly the *Tjeker* of Egyptian sources with the Šikalayū of Ugarit. The *tj* of *Tjeker* should be phoneticized *s* (samakh); and, of course, Egyptian *r* can equal *r* or *l* in Semitic. The gentilic Šikalayū actually masks the ethnicon Šikil (see Rainey, "Toponymic Problems," *Tel Aviv* 9 [1982], p. 134; for the best interpretation of the text, see Gregory Mobley, "The Identity of the Šikalayū [RS 34.129]," *BASOR* [forthcoming].

Thus the Sea Peoples, who established themselves at Dor in the early 12th century B.C.—namely, the *Sikils*—closely resemble the *Sikeloi* of later Greek sources, the people who gave their name to Sicily, just as the *Sherden*, another group of Sea Peoples, bequeathed their name to Sardinia, and the *Teresh/Tursha* to first Tarsus and later to the Etruscans of Italy. According to the dispersal of proper names and the evidence of immigrant Mycenaeans, it would appear that during the "colonization" of the coastal Levant and Cyprus, fissiparous groups of Sea Peoples bearing the same ethnicons settled the coastal regions of the central Mediterranean and bequeathed their names to several peoples and places there.

[24] Moshe Dothan, "Archaeological Evidence for Movements" and his "Sardina at Akko?" in *Studies in Sardinian Archaeology: Sardinia in the Mediterranean*, vol. 2, ed. Miriam Balmuth (Ann Arbor: Univ. of Michigan Press, 1986), pp. 105-115.

[25] Avraham Biran, "The Collared-rim Jars and the Settlement of the Tribe of Dan," in Gitin and Dever, *Recent Excavation*, pp. 71-96.

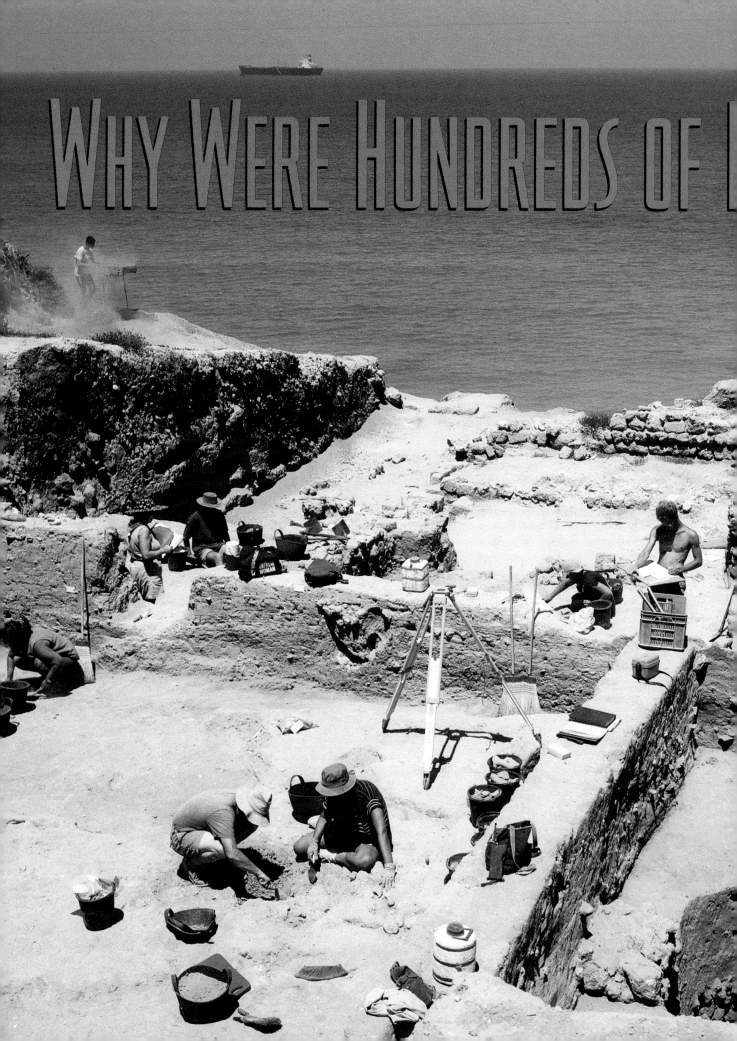

GS BURIED AT ASHKELON?

Ancient Ashkelon, now quietly nestled beside the Mediterranean in the south of Israel, is shaped like a giant 150-acre bowl, with the sea wearing away at much of the western half. The rim and sides of the bowl are formed by the mammoth Middle Bronze Age glacis, or rampart, that once protected the city. Inside the bowl are buried at least 20 ancient cities, dating from about 3500 B.C. to 1500 A.D., a span of 5,000 years.

In Part I we examined the Middle Bronze and Iron Age cities—the first, Canaanite and the second, Philistine.

In 604 B.C., Philistine Ashkelon was destroyed by the neo-Babylonian king Nebuchadrezzar (neb-uh-kuh-DREZ-uhr; also called Nebuchadnezzar [neb-uh-kuhd-NEZ-uhr]), whose army soon thereafter (in 586 B.C.) destroyed Jerusalem, capital of the kingdom of Judah, together with its Temple. Thus began what is known in Israelite history as the

Preceding pages: *A modern-day tanker (upper left) plies the calm waters of the Mediterranean as excavators in the foreground navigate towards the past. Their site along Ashkelon's coast was home during the late-sixth and fifth centuries B.C., first, to an approximately 30-by 60-foot port warehouse and then, for about 50 years, to a huge dog cemetery (the inset shows a typical dog burial; see p. 27 for more information on the practice). In all, excavators have uncovered at least six phases, totaling 10 feet in thickness, of Persian-period (538-332 B.C.) occupational debris in Ashkelon atop the earlier Philistine (12th-7th centuries B.C.) phase of occupation.*

Starting about 500 B.C., the Mediterranean coast enjoyed a burst of prosperity under Persian-appointed Phoenician rulers. Author Lawrence E. Stager, who heads the excavations at Ashkelon and who in Part I described the earlier history of the city under the Canaanites and the Philistines, here moves the story forward into the Persian period, a time when Ashkelon was a city of cultural diversity, teeming with Phoenicians, Greeks, Persians and Egyptians. He also unveils a challenging new hypothesis on why so many dogs were buried on prime seaside real estate.

Babylonian Exile. Less widely known is the fact that the Philistines too were exiled to Babylon.

The Babylonians were replaced (in 538 B.C.) by the Persians, who expanded and then ruled the biggest empire the world had known before Alexander the Great—from the eastern Mediterranean to India. A more benign imperial power than the Babylonians—perhaps we may even characterize their hegemony as enlightened—the Persians under Cyrus the Great allowed the Jews to return to their land and even to rebuild their Temple (Ezra 1:2-4, 6:3-5).

No record exists, however, as to what happened to the exiled Philistines. Those who may have remained in Ashkelon after Nebuchadrezzar's conquest apparently lost their ethnic identity. They simply disappear from history.

Culturally, Ashkelon once again became Canaanite—or, more precisely, Phoenician, as the coastal Canaanites are called at this time, having developed a culture of their own, supported by a far-flung commercial empire to the west.

During the Persian period (538-332 B.C.), the great Persian kings ruled the area politically, but they were not cultural imperialists. Even politically, they ruled with a comparatively gentle hand, giving rather wide latitude to local satrapies. In the heart of Phoenicia—the eastern Mediterranean coast, in what today is Lebanon—the Persians found willing allies among the Phoenicians, who provided their Persian overlords with naval power and wealth from the Mediterranean world and beyond.

For their cooperation, the Persians gave Phoenicians from Sidon and Tyre control of the coast as far south as Ashkelon. (Farther south, Gaza remained more a desert port than a Mediterranean seaport.) The Persians assigned governors for the coastal cities, cleverly alternating a Tyrian and a Sidonian governor for each major coastal city down to Ashkelon. According to a mid-to-late-fourth-century B.C. source,[1] Ashkelon was known as a "city of the Tyrians" and headquarters of a Tyrian governor.

Phoenician culture—and therefore, we may assume, the Phoenicians—dominated Ashkelon by the late sixth or early fifth century B.C. This is evidenced by Phoenician inscriptions (one as early as about 500 B.C.), iconography characteristic of Phoenician religion (especially the sign of the goddess Tanit [see p. 31]) and by the Phoenician pottery we excavated.

The Phoenicians brought with them to Ashkelon

Surrounded by their tools, *two excavators gingerly uncover a fifth-century B.C. Phoenician transport amphora (used primarily to carry wine or oil) within a warehouse along Ashkelon's coast (see p. 26).*

CARL ANDREWS

not only their culture. With their maritime and commercial skills, they also brought a great deal of prosperity to the port. In fact, the whole eastern coast of the Mediterranean prospered during the Persian period under the enterprising Phoenicians. This stands in sharp contrast to the comparatively impoverished province of Judah, or Yehud (ye-HOOD) as it was known in official Aramaic in the Persian period, with Jerusalem as its capital. In abundance of Persian-period remains, the contrast between the two areas is remarkable. Inland, in Yehud, Persian-period strata are very thin if not ephemeral. On the Mediterranean coast, Persian-period occupational debris is quite thick—6 to 10 feet at Ashkelon and at Dor to the north.

Within the huge bowl that is the tell at Ashkelon are two mounds, one in the northern part and one in the southern part of the site. On the north side of the southern mound (Grid 38), known as al-Hadra, nearly 10 feet of Persian-period occupational debris overlay the Philistine strata. The Persian-period sequence begins with monumental ashlar* buildings that we have only partially excavated. Thereafter, we found at least five more phases** or subphases of buildings, culminating in a major destruction in about 300 B.C. Rooms in the destroyed buildings were filled with burnt and fallen debris from the superstructure. In the debris were buried basket-handled amphorae (AM-fo-ree)† and a linen bag filled with Phoenician silver coins of the fourth century B.C.

* Ashlars are well-cut masonry in the shape of a cube.

** We have not yet assigned site-wide strata numbers to the various phases within local grids (100 meters by 100 meters). Phase numbers apply only within each grid. The phase numbers are not necessarily the same from grid to grid, although eventually we may determine they are part of the same stratum.

† An amphora (sing., AM-fo-ruh) is a large storage jar.

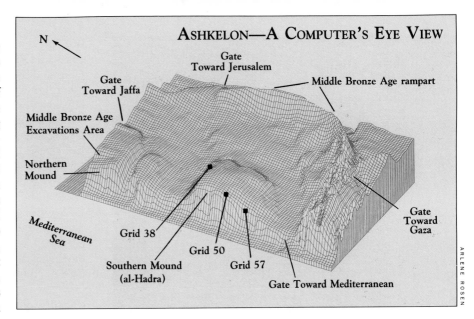

ASHKELON—A COMPUTER'S EYE VIEW

Gate Toward Jerusalem

Gate Toward Jaffa

Middle Bronze Age rampart

Middle Bronze Age Excavations Area

Northern Mound

Mediterranean Sea

Grid 38

Grid 50

Grid 57

Southern Mound (al-Hadra)

Gate Toward Gaza

Gate Toward Mediterranean

ARLENE ROSEN

Flying the friendly skies *over Ashkelon, thanks to modern technology. This topographic map, generated by a computer program that renders elevation measurements into graphic form, shows the important features of the city as they would have appeared from a hypothetical point above the Mediterranean. The small squares are a function of the program and do not relate to excavation squares. Though Ashkelon did drop precipitously to the sea along its western edge, the sudden drop here along the northern and southern sides is a result of the computer's truncation of the view.*

That the conflagration was widespread is clear from evidence in Grid 57 on the southwestern side of the city. Here we found the same phases and subphases of Persian-period occupation, beginning with a monumental structure built in about 500 B.C., followed by later phases of architecture, such as street-front workshops, culminating in a massive destruction. Shortly before the destruction of about 300 B.C., the inhabitants of one of the buildings secreted a hoard of silver coins and a silver bracelet. The coins were tetradrachmas (tet-ruh-DRAK-muhs) bearing the portrait of Alexander the Great. Nearby was a laurel-leaf crown of gold with

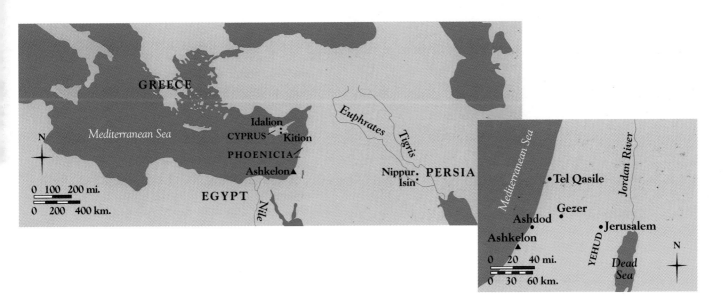

GREECE

Mediterranean Sea

Idalion
CYPRUS Kition
PHOENICIA
Ashkelon

Euphrates

Tigris

Nippur
Isin PERSIA

EGYPT

Nile

0 100 200 mi.
0 200 400 km.

Mediterranean Sea

Tel Qasile

Gezer

Ashdod

Ashkelon

Jerusalem

Jordan River

YEHUD

Dead Sea

0 20 40 mi.
0 30 60 km.

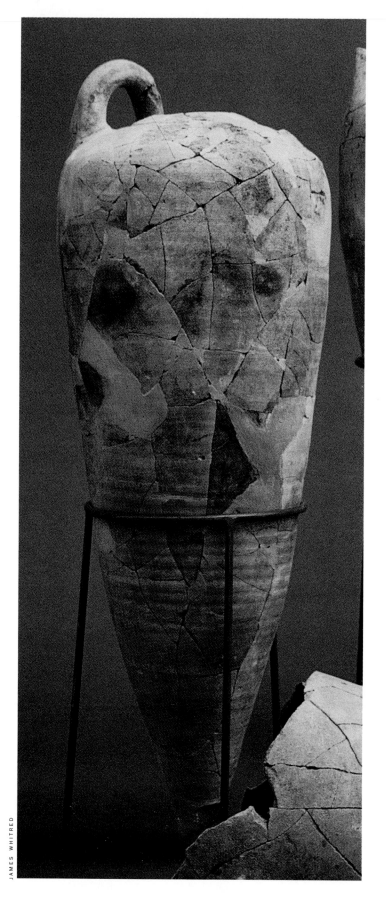

A large basket-handled amphora *from the fourth century B.C. and imported to Ashkelon from Cyprus or Rhodes. The pointed bases of such amphorae could be inserted into clay pot stands or stuck into sand or soil.*

JAMES WHITRED

side pieces of gilded bone. Several basket-handled amphorae stored on the second floor of one of the buildings collapsed onto the first floor. The basement was filled with burnt bricks, rubble and pottery of the late fourth century B.C.

Because of the presence of a hoard of his coins, the citywide destruction must have occurred after Alexander the Great (356-323 B.C.) had conquered the Levant (about 332 B.C.). Ashkelon (but not Gaza) was apparently spared the destruction which accompanied Alexander's conquest. But soon thereafter, in about 300 B.C. (although we cannot be certain until all of the data—pottery, coins, etc.—have been analyzed), Ashkelon too was devastated. This tragic episode must have occurred about the time Ptolemy I Soter (c. 367/6-283/2 B.C.) of Egypt was establishing his supremacy over the region, when Ashkelon was no longer under the control of Tyre.

In Grid 57 we also made one of the strangest discoveries of the entire excavation. In the phase following the construction of the monumental building mentioned previously, sandwiched in between that initial phase and the following architectural phase was a brief interlude (Phase 5 in Grid 57) when the floor area was leveled and used as a dog cemetery! We found a dozen dogs carefully buried here.

In nearby Grid 50 we uncovered an impressive building with six almost identical rooms. These rooms seem to be magazines of a large warehouse, about 30 by 60 feet. Each magazine had nearly 250 square feet of interior storage space. On the floors of the magazines, we excavated several Phoenician amphorae; Greek Attic Black-glazed ware; Red-figured as well as Black-figured fine ware, also from Greece; and a scapula (collar-bone) of a camel that was one of the basic raw materials from which fine bone artifacts were manufactured. The imprint of a basket containing red ocher was all that remained of perishable items. Other pigments, such as brown umber from Cyprus, were found stored nearby.

In its original construction, this large warehouse was stepped or terraced down toward the sea; the western half of the building's stone foundations therefore lay at a lower level than the eastern half. In the next phase (Phase 7 in Grid 50, which corresponds to Phase 5 in Grid 57), this western area was leveled up with a series of rubbish-laden fills. But before the leveled area was next used as a warehouse (sometime in the last half of the fifth century B.C.), the deeper fills above the western half of the warehouse were put to a far different use: it was part of a huge dog cemetery that extended all the way to the 12 dog burials we had found in Grid 57. Moreover, the western limits of the dog cemetery could not be ascertained because that part had eroded into the sea.

Till now, we have found more than 700 partial or complete dog carcasses from the fifth century B.C., most of them buried in the western half of Grid 50. Because only the eastern limits of this dog cemetery have been established, we can speculate that it was originally much larger, with dog burials probably numbering in the thousands. This is by far the largest dog cemetery of any kind known in the ancient world.

Ashkelon's dog cemetery was of extremely short duration, perhaps lasting no more than 50 years. Thereafter the area was returned to its previous mercantile use (though we have indications that dogs still received special burials elsewhere later in the Persian period). Nevertheless, in that short period, as many as three burials were found superimposed in some places, one dug into the other. This suggests that there were no burial markers over the graves.

Each dog carcass was carefully and individually placed in a shallow pit dug into the fill of what had previously been a warehouse. Each dog was deliberately placed on its side, its legs flexed and its tail tucked in around the hindlegs. The carcass was then carefully covered with earth containing a mixture of cultural debris. However, no grave goods can be associated with the dog burials.

When undisturbed by later building activity or scavenging, the dog burials present a remarkably homogeneous picture. Actually, it was quite tedious (some would say boring) excavating them, each of which we had to excavate as carefully as the last.

About 60 to 70 percent of the dogs were puppies; the remainder were subadult and adult dogs. Our staff zooarchaeologists, Dr. Paula Wapnish and Professor Brian Hesse, of the University of Alabama in Birmingham,

Ashkelon's treasures. *Silver tetradrachma coins bearing the portrait of Alexander the Great on one side and depicting him on the other as Zeus holding a scepter in his left hand and an eagle in his right, and a silver bracelet (right), as well as a laurel-leaf crown of gold with side pieces of gilded bone (below) were found among the charred debris of a building along Ashkelon's coast. The structure was destroyed in a citywide conflagration in about 300 B.C., when Ptolemy I Soter of Egypt was establishing his rule over the region.*

ILAN SZTULMAN

CARL ANDREWS

tell us that the skeletons lack any butchering marks, which indicates that the dogs died of natural causes. This is confirmed, according to them, by the fact that the mortality profile of the Ashkelon dogs is similar to that of urban dog populations today. Thus, it does not appear that these dogs were eaten (as the Persians accused the Phoenician Carthaginians of doing[2]). Nor does it appear that these dogs were offered as sacrifices, despite the implication in Third Isaiah* in a passage written shortly before the Ashkelon dog cemetery was established:

> "Whoever slaughters an ox is like one who kills a human being; whoever sacrifices a lamb, like one who breaks a dog's neck; whoever presents a grain offering, like one who offers swine's blood; whoever makes a memorial offering of frankincense, like one who blesses an idol." (Isaiah 66:3; New RSV)

The mature Ashkelon dogs were a little over 20 inches

(text continues on p. 32)

* The Book of Isaiah was written by different prophets at different times. Chapters 1-39 are pre-Exilic; that is, before the Babylonian Exile. The remainder (chapters 40-66) is post-Exilic; it is attributed either to an anonymous Second Isaiah (deutero-Isaiah) or, in the opinion of some scholars, chapters 40-59 to Second Isaiah and chapters 60-66 to Third Isaiah (trito-Isaiah).

Mediterranean traders *brought their goods to Ashkelon's Persian-period port warehouse, outlined in the plan at right. (The solid lines on the plan indicate extant walls; dashed lines represent reconstructed walls.) Its six rooms, each about 12 by 27 feet, contained pottery imported from throughout the Mediterranean. The large hole at lower right in the photo is the test trench dug by British archaeologist W. Phythian-Adams in 1921; the smaller round holes are Byzantine-period wells.*

Because the area where the warehouse stood dropped noticeably down to the sea, the foundation of the western half of the building lay lower than the eastern side. Sometime in the first half of the fifth century B.C., the western side was filled in to make it level with the eastern side. Before a warehouse could be rebuilt at the site, however, it was put to a puzzling new use: a vast dog cemetery (found in the area of the upper portion of the photo), somehow related to ancient religious practices.

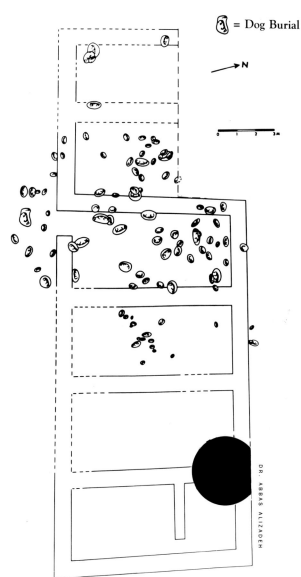

(X) = Dog Burial

→N

ERICH LESSING

A Phoenician's best friend. *In the first half of the fifth century B.C., the area around the port warehouse underwent a dramatic change: it was turned into a huge dog cemetery—the largest uncovered anywhere in the ancient world. Seven hundred dog skeletons have been unearthed so far, all of them originally buried like the female and puppy shown at top: laid on their sides in a shallow pit, with legs flexed and tails tucked around the hindlegs. The western portion of the cemetery has been washed into the sea, leading excavators to believe that even more dogs—perhaps thousands—were once buried here.*

A sleek hunting dog in the photo above, from the so-called Alexander Sarcophagus, approximates the size and shape of the dogs buried at Ashkelon. The dramatic scene is part of a series depicting Alexander the Great and the client-king of Phoenicia engaging in a hunt and is now on display in the

Archaeological Museum in Istanbul, Turkey.

The dogs—whose closest modern counterpart is the Bedouin sheepdog known as the Palestinian pariah dog—died of natural causes, were of medium height and build and had a mortality profile (60 to 70 per cent of them were puppies) similar to urban dog populations today. The dogs, therefore, were not sacrificed as part of a ritual, nor were they eaten. Excavators puzzled over why the people of Persian-period Ashkelon would have gone to such lengths to bury so many ordinary-seeming dogs. Author Stager suggests the dogs were part of a healing cult, perhaps associated with the Phoenician god Resheph-Mukol. This or a similar cult led Deuteronomy 23:18 to declare: "You shall not bring the hire of a harlot, or the wages of a dog [paid for healing services] into the house of the Lord your god in payment for any vow; for both of these are an abomination to the Lord your God."

ILAN SZTULMAN

The imprint of Greek culture. *The Greek legacy abounds in Persian-period Ashkelon, as the pictures on these pages attest. An owl, symbol of the Greek goddess Athena, stares intently from the side of a fifth-century B.C. Attic Red-figured cup (above; Attica was the region in Greece where Athens is located) found in the warehouse shown on page 26. Another fifth-century Attic item, part of a wine krater, or large jar, can be seen opposite, top far right. Other signs of Greek influence in Ashkelon include a fourth-century B.C. South Italic Red-figured vase (below), made by potters living in Greek colonies in Italy; a fourth-century B.C. Attic Black-glazed bowl (near right, center); and the limestone head of a youth in Cypro-Classical style, probably imported from Cyprus in the fifth century B.C. (near right, top).*

TERRY SMITH

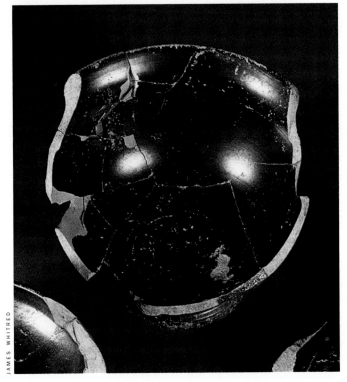

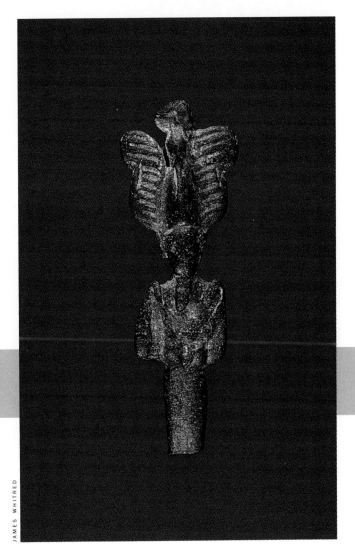

Egyptian Cultural Influence ▶

A crown sits atop the head of the Egyptian deity Osiris, king of the dead and the underworld, in this bronze figurine from the fourth century B.C. (right). Though Ashkelon was receptive to Egyptian culture and though Egyptians venerated dogs, it is not likely that the vast dog cemetery is related to Egyptian cult practices; most tellingly, the dogs of Ashkelon were not mummified, as were most canines ritually buried by the Egyptians.

CARL ANDREWS

DR. ABBAS ALIZADEH

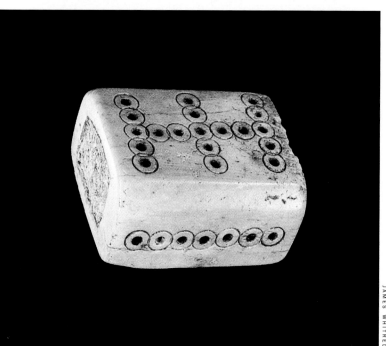

JAMES WHITRED

Persian presence. *Shown here are residues of sixth-through fourth-century B.C. Persian culture in Ashkelon. Despite the fact that this is called the Persian period, Persian culture was nevertheless relatively scant, especially compared to remains reflecting Phoenician culture. One important indicator of a Persian presence is an exquisitely carved ivory comb (above left and artist's rendition above) showing a hunter on horseback (note that he sits on a decorated horseblanket and not in a saddle and that the stirrup had not yet been invented). Below the horse is a reclining ibex; two lions march across the register at bottom. The other side of the comb (not shown) shows two men thrusting swords into a lion. Though the top of the comb is broken off and the edges had been pared down in antiquity, Dr. Abbas Alizadeh has reconstructed the original scene using contemporary Persian iconography. The domino-like object (left) is a Persian scale weight consisting of an incised bone case and a lead filling. It dates to the fifth century B.C. and weighs one karsha, a Persian unit of weight and value equal to ten shekels of silver.*

CARL ANDREWS

Phoenician emblems. *The fifth-century B.C. human-like stick figures above, in bone (far right) and bronze, are known as "the sign of Tanit." An important member of the Phoenician pantheon, the goddess Tanit was especially popular on stelae in the vast precinct of child sacrifice in Phoenician/Punic Carthage (eighth to second centuries B.C.). Tanit is often identified with the mother goddess Asherah; her consort, Baal Hammon, was a leading deity in Carthage. Coins from Roman-period Ashkelon indicate that Tanit's temple in the city continued to attract worshippers throughout the Roman period (first century B.C.-fourth century A.D.).*

Other Persian-period items uncovered in Ashkelon include a ceramic blowfish, its piscine lips puckered (right) and a carved ivory knife handle in the shape of a crouching bull (bottom right), both dating to the fourth century B.C. Though only about three-quarters of an inch high, the fifth-century B.C. stamp seal (below) of a hero fighting a lion (found at Ashkelon's warehouse) displays the influences of two cultures. The pose is a common one in Persian art, but the hero's short skirt is Phoenician. These items, and the transport amphora (p. 22), testify to the dominance of Phoenician culture in Ashkelon.

JAMES WHITRED

CARL ANDREWS

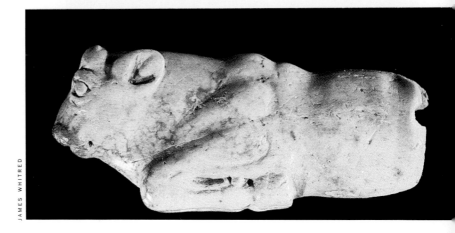

JAMES WHITRED

(continued from p. 26)

high and weighed a little more than 30 pounds—a dog population of medium height and build. Although no known modern breed correlates exactly with the Ashkelon dogs, Wapnish and Hesse have found a modern counterpart in today's Bedouin sheepdogs, known as Palestinian pariah dogs. The best ancient representation of dogs similar to the Ashkelon dogs is probably the hound on the so-called Alexander Sarcophagus (late fourth century B.C.) from Sidon, on which Alexander the Great and his client, the king of Sidon, pursue a lion with a hunting hound of about the same size and build as the Ashkelon dogs. Like the dog on the sarcophagus, the Ashkelon hounds could have been used in hunting, to pursue hares, gazelles, wild goats or even lions.

A critical datum: Newborn dogs and puppies were given the same careful mortuary treatment as more mature dogs. This concern for the proper burial of what in some cases were probably dog fetuses reflects an intense relationship between dogs and humans. Yet, because many of these dogs lived only for a short time, if at all, the attachment could not be based on mere companionship.

In classical Greek society, where dogs were greatly appreciated, poets sometimes wrote very moving epitaphs for dogs, to be inscribed on markers over the pet's grave, as in this example penned by the poet Tymnes in about 300 B.C.:

Three men and an inscription. *Frank Moore Cross (center) deciphers a bowl inscribed in fifth-century Phoenician, discovered in the dog cemetery at Ashkelon, though not in a dog burial. Flanking him are Leon Levy (right), connoisseur of ancient Near Eastern art, philanthropist and patron of the Ashkelon expedition, and Lawrence E. Stager, head of the excavations. The bowl had two holes drilled above its inscription so that it could be displayed on a wall by means of a leather thong. The inscription contains a word that Cross reads as ʿgm, "cakes." Intriguingly, honey- and cheese-cakes were a common offering in the healing cult of Asklepios, either to the deity or to the sacred dogs associated with him.*

"The stone tells that it [the grave] contains here the white Milesian dog, Eumelos' faithful guardian. They called him 'Bull' while he still lived, but now the silent paths of night possess his voice."[3]

But in ancient Greece, as now, special burials were reserved for pets old enough for some kind of human bonding to have occurred. This could not have been the case for the majority of dogs buried at Ashkelon.

The best explanation seems to be that the Ashkelon dogs were revered as sacred animals. As such, they were probably associated with a particular deity and with that god's sacred precinct, about which the dogs were free to roam.

I hasten to add that we have not yet found a shrine or temple associated with the dog cemetery. But most of the environs of the cemetery have not yet been excavated—and a substantial area to the west has collapsed into the sea.

The area occupied by the dog cemetery is significant. Throughout the preceding and the remainder of the Persian period, this ground was devoted to profit-making enterprises connected with the export-import business. But for a generation or so, this was interrupted by the dog cemetery, apparently devoted to ritual purposes.

Dog burials are extremely rare outside of Ashkelon, although in the same period at neighboring Ashdod, seven dog burials were recorded. Recently, a dog from the Persian period was found buried in a jar at Tell Qasile, in modern Tel Aviv.[4] Several dogs were also found buried at Gezer, but these are a couple of centuries later, in the Hellenistic period.

Like many other ports and caravan cities, Ashkelon had a heterogeneous population throughout most of its history, comprised of local citizens and a variety of foreign merchants. In cosmopolitan Ashkelon of the Persian period, we should not be surprised to find Persians, Phoenicians, Philistines, Egyptians, Greeks and Jews. And the artifacts recovered in our excavations provide evidence for the presence of diverse elements in the city's population from the mid-sixth through the fourth centuries B.C. The culture of any of these could provide clues to understanding the significance of the strange dog cemetery we found in the midst of this mercantile district.

In the cosmology of the Persian Zoroastrians, dogs rank next to humans in both this world and the next. In Zoroastrian death rites, the priest gives an egg, a symbol of immortality, to a dog to eat. He then leads the dog to the home of the dead person, where the dog gazes at the corpse and then eats three pieces of bread from the chest of the corpse. After that, the dead body is washed and shrouded. Then for three days a dog vicariously eats three meals a day for the deceased. Then each day for the next 40 days, the canine vicar is fed three pieces of baked bread and a roasted egg at the house of the deceased.[5]

Although Persian reverence for dogs might have influenced the practice at Ashkelon, a Zoroastrian would not have laid the corpse of a human or a dog directly in the ground without a lining of stones or the like to protect the earth from the corpse, which was considered a highly charged pollutant.[6] That the dogs in the Ashkelon cemetery were placed directly into the ground in unlined pits mitigates against the Zoroastrian association.

Moreover, the traces of Persian material culture in the West are minimal. At Ashkelon a beautiful ivory comb, with hunting scenes and rows of lions, recalls Persian Achaemenid art; a lead weight encased in a truncated shaft of decorated bone seems to conform to the Persian standard (see p. 30 for these items).[7] But other than that, the immediate, direct impact of Persians on the material culture of the coast seems negligible.

What about the Egyptians? We know that the Egyptians were nearby and exported basketfuls of trinkets and amulets to Ashkelon (see p. 29). The Egyptians are well known for their reverence, even worship, of animals: they installed them in temples and devoted spe-

cial precincts to their burials, although most were mummified for careers in the afterlife. Diodorus Siculus, writing in the first century B.C., mentions the dog among several animals venerated by Egyptians:

> "For each kind of animal [including dogs] that is accorded this worship there has been consecrated a portion of land which returns a revenue sufficient for their care and sustenance. . . .
>
> "The sacred animals are kept in 'sacred enclosures' and are cared for by many men of distinction who offer them the most expensive fare. . . . When one of these animals dies, they wrap it in fine linen and then, wailing and beating their breasts, carry it off to be embalmed . . ., [and then] they lay it away in a consecrated tomb."[8]

None of the buried dogs at Ashkelon, however, showed any signs of mummification.

Thus, although the Greeks, Egyptians and Persians could all be described as "canidophiles" (dog-lovers), I doubt that any one of these relatively small ethnic groups residing in Ashkelon could have accounted for the hundreds (if not thousands) of dogs buried here in the fifth century B.C. And neither the Greeks nor the Egyptians would have had the authority to convert prime real estate into a sacred precinct for dog burials.

The only people with sufficient authority and a large enough population to account for so many dog burials in such a short time were the Phoenicians. Their material culture dominated Ashkelon throughout the Persian period. This is shown by the ubiquity of their religious symbols, such as the "sign of Tanit" (see p. 31), as well as their pottery and inscriptions. Although other ethnic groups, such as the Egyptians or the Persians, might have had an influence on Phoenician attitudes and ritual concerning dogs, it was the Phoenicians, I believe, who were responsible for the dog burials at Ashkelon and who considered the dog a sacred animal. The evidence for this inference—derived mainly from the archaeological remains—is, however, not conclusive. I describe it in some detail in the box on the following pages.

Presumably the dog became associated with healing because of the curative powers evident from licking its own wounds or sores. One neo-Assyrian text in cuneiform suggests that even touching the sacred dog was sufficient to heal: "If a man goes to the temple of his god, and if he touches . . .(?), he is clean (again?); likewise if he touches the dog of Gula [the goddess of healing], he is clean (again?)."[9]

Dogs were involved in healing cults in many different cultures in antiquity; their association with temples and healing deities was rather widespread in the ancient Mediterranean and Near Eastern worlds, whether it be Gula in Mesopotamia, Asklepios in Greece, Eshmun in Phoenicia, Mukol or Resheph-Mukol in Phoenician Cyprus, or, earlier still, at Late Bronze Age Beth-Shean. In Egypt sacred dogs participated in rituals where, according to Diodorus, the Egyptians "make vows to certain gods on behalf of their children who have been delivered from an illness, in which case they shave off

(text continues on p. 36)

DEITIES AND DOGS—THEIR SACRED RITES

In the ancient Near East, dogs are often associated with particular deities and the powers they wield. We cannot yet be sure with which deity the dogs in the cemetery at Ashkelon were associated. There are several possibilities, in several cultural guises, often interrelated as one deity merges into another.

But in the end, a common theme emerges—deities with healing powers are often associated with dogs.

According to a Phoenician legend, the leading deity of the city of Tyre, Herakles-Melkart, was credited with the discovery of purple. Actually, however, it was his dog who discovered the product for which the Phoenicians were world-renowned—purple dye, extracted from a gland in a Murex mollusk: Herakles was strolling along the beach with his dog and with a beautiful nymph named Tyrus. His hound discovered a Murex and bit into it. The dye from the snail stained the dog's lips a bright purple, a color the nymph greatly admired. Herakles collected enough mollusks to dye a robe purple and presented this fine gift to the nymph. This discovery was celebrated on coins from Tyre, depicting a dog sniffing a Murex snail.[1]

More pertinent, however, is a small (about 6 by 4 inches) mid-fifth-century B.C. limestone plaque inscribed on both sides in Phoenician; it was found in 1869 at the Phoenician port city of Kition on Cyprus.[2]

The Kition plaque lists personnel associated in some way with the temples of the goddess of fertility, Astarte, and a more obscure male deity, Mukol (vocalized variously as Mekal, Mukal or even Mikal). Mukol appears as part of a compound god name, Resheph-Mukol (*ršpmkl*) in several fourth-century B.C. inscriptions at Idalion, Cyprus, where his cult flourished.[3] In a trilingual inscription from there,[4] Resheph-Mukol is equated in Greek with Apollo-Amuklos.

Resheph is known from Ugaritic and Aramaic inscriptions as the lord of the underworld (= Mesopotamian Nergal), lord of plague, pestilence and disease—and conversely the god of healing. William F. Albright suggested that the Phoenician god of healing *par excellence*, Eshmun (whose Greek equivalent was Asklepios), had a Canaanite precursor, Šulman (literally, "One of welfare"). The Canaanite underworld figure named Rašap-Šulman, then, represented both polarities, namely sickness and health.[5]

Resheph-Mukol = Apollo-Amuklos could be the same sort of bipolar deity, embodying what seems to us (but not to them) mutually exclusive, contradictory aspects. At Ugarit, Resheph bore the title "Lord of the Arrow Resheph" (*bʿl ḥz ršp*). A millennium later in Cyprus he was still called "Resheph of the Arrow."[6] The name itself probably means "Burning"/"Fever"/"Plague" according to Frank Moore Cross.

Apollo also has an ambivalent nature: besides being a god of healing, father of Asklepios and bearing the epithet Physician (*Iatros*), Apollo is also the god of plague. In the *Iliad* I.43-52 an angry Apollo marches down from Mt. Olympus, carrying his silver bow, the arrows rattling in his quiver. He sends a plague upon the Achaean army by shooting a "tearing arrow" into them. "The corpse fires burned everywhere and did not stop burning." For nine days Apollo bombarded them with arrows. As William J. Fulco and Walter Burkert so astutely pointed out, the "arrows of Apollo," like those of Resheph (and we might add, those of Yahweh), signify pestilence.[7] Conversely, Apollo's image was capable of warding off plague. It was Canaanite Resheph-Mukal who bequeathed many attributes to the archer-god Apollo, god of healing, god of plague.

There may be a much earlier evidence of the bipolar Resheph-Mukol, or Mukal, in Late Bronze Age Beth-Shean. An Egyptian stela found there in a temple from stratum IX depicts a bearded deity who sits enthroned before two worshippers.[8] The deity wears a high conical cap with two streamers down the back and two small horns protruding from the front—horns very much like those worn by Resheph, whose animal emblems included the gazelle. However, the seated deity is identified by the hieroglyphic inscription as "Mukal, the great god, lord of Beth-Shean." From the same temple of Mukal comes one of the most superb pieces of Canaanite art, a beautifully carved basalt relief (probably an orthostat), 3 feet high, with the following scene: In the upper register a dog and a lion stand on their hindlegs engaged in battle. In the lower one, the dog is prevailing over the lion as he bites the haunches of the lion. It is tempting to link the victorious dog with the god Mukal.

It seems clear that the Greek Apollo

BRITISH MUSEUM

The Kition plaque. *This mid-fifth-century B.C. limestone plaque was discovered in 1869 in Kition, Cyprus, once a great Phoenician port. Inscribed in black ink in Phoenician, both sides of the plaque list personnel associated with the temples of Astarte, the goddess of fertility, and the lesser-known plague and healing god Mukol. Included among the temple personnel listed are klbm (dogs) and grm, a much-disputed term. Author Stager believes the latter means puppies and argues that the Kition plaque provides an account contemporaneous to the Ashkelon dog cemetery of dogs and puppies employed in a Phoenician healing cult.*

inherited his darker side as god of pestilence as well as his brighter side as god of healing from Canaanite Resheph. It was this Apollo of Cypro-Phoenician lineage who bequeathed his name to the Roman city Apollonia, between Caesarea and Jaffa, which earlier had been named for Resheph, as the modern Arabic place-name Arsuf still attests. Likewise, the worship of Apollo in Hellenistic Ashkelon probably bore more resemblance to that of Resheph-Mukol in Phoenician Cyprus than to the sun worship and youth cult of Apollo in Greece. One tradition has it that Herod's grandfather served as hierodule (a temple servant) in the temple of Apollo at Ashkelon. The sacred dogs of Ashkelon, like the dogs and puppies at Kition, just might have been part of a healing cult in the tradition of Apollo-Resheph-Mukol.*

By classical times in Greece, Asklepios, the son of Apollo (= Resheph), had become more popular among the Greeks than even his father Apollo, also a healing deity. The most famous shrine of Asklepios' healing cult was at Epidaurus, where patients would come to spend the night in the dormitory (abaton) in the hope that Asklepios would appear to them in a dream vision and reveal a cure for the sleeper's disease or illness. Or the clients might be visited during the night by surrogates of the god—sacred dogs and snakes whose "tongues" were believed to have a therapeutic effect on the clients. Professor Howard Clark Kee of Boston University provides this memorable image of the experience: "It is easy to imagine the vigil of the suppliants, lying in the total darkness of the abaton, listening for the padding feet of the priests or the sacred dogs, or the nearly noiseless slithering of the sacred snakes."[9]

Among the temple personnel mentioned on the Kition plaque are builders, marshals, singers, servants, sacrificers, bakers, barbers, shepherds (who may have raised flocks for temple sacrifices), maidens ('lmt, sometimes rendered "temple prostitutes") and—relevant to our topic—dogs (klbm). In short, here we find dogs associated with a Phoenician temple, or temples, of Astarte and Mukol.

All of the personnel mentioned in the Kition plaque, including dogs, receive particular payments for services rendered.

* As we shall see in Part III, there were other Phoenician deities and their cults, such as Tanit and her temple, which persisted right on through Roman times, sometimes under a new Greek or Latin name.

The word "dogs" appears in the same line of this inscription with a much-disputed term, grm. According to one scholar, A. Van den Branden, the dogs were actually humans who served as male prostitutes, or sodomites, in the temple rituals. This is the service for which they were paid. The grm, according to Van den Branden, were "lambs" or "adolescent prostitutes" in the cult. Later he modified his interpretation and suggested that these two groups of temple prostitutes received their names—"dogs" and "lambs"—from the animal masks and costumes they wore.[10] The masked humans symbolized an earlier era when bestiality, involving real dogs and lambs, was performed in the cult.

Van den Branden based his (mis)understanding of the text on the Kition plaque largely on a common but equally questionable interpretation of a Biblical text, Deuteronomy 23:18:

"You shall not bring the hire of a harlot, or the wages of a dog into the house of the Lord your god in payment for any vow; for both of these are an abomination to the Lord your God."

Van den Branden's argument is based in large part on this passage from Deuteronomy, in which most Biblical commentators contend that "wages of a dog" is parallel to "hire of a harlot"; a harlot (zonah) being a female prostitute, dog (klb) must, therefore, be a male prostitute.

I do not see the necessity, however, of assuming that "dog" in this passage is the male counterpart of a female prostitute. It is not sodomy or pederasty that is the abomination in the context of this passage; rather it is the "bad" money accruing from the services of a harlot or a dog. To use that kind of money to pay for a vow in the Jerusalem Temple would be an abomination to the Israelite deity Yahweh.

Professor Brian Peckham of the University of Toronto, an expert on the Phoenicians, has written a superb analysis of the Kition plaque in which he too discards connotations of sodomy and pederasty that some scholars have imputed to the terms klbm (dogs) and grm in the Kition plaque. He has also decisively dated the Kition plaque to about 450 B.C., precisely in our period. On the other hand, Peckham agrees with Van den Branden that the dogs (klbm) and grm were humans masked as animals, who participated in some kind of temple rituals. The people with klbm masks were masquerading as dogs; those with grm

A dog and a lion (right and left, respectively) do battle on the top register of a 3-foot-high basalt relief from Late Bronze Age Beth-Shean. In the lower register the dog seems to be vanquishing his foe, biting the haunches of the lion. Author Stager suggests that the dog in this relief may represent Mukal in his aspect of god of healing.

masks, as lions. The latter identification is based on the Hebrew gr (plural, grm) which means lions or, more precisely, lion cubs, since Hebrew grm usually refers to lion whelps in the Bible.[11]

I prefer, however, to take a very literal interpretation of klb (dog; plural klbm) in both Deuteronomy 23:18 and in the Kition plaque. In both texts the authors are referring not to humans acting like dogs in cult dramas but to actual dogs that performed services in the sacred precincts of the Phoenicians. Moreover, grm (singular gr) in the Bible can refer not only to lion whelps but also to the young of any animal, such as the jackal in Lamentations 4:3; on this basis the grm in the Kition plaque refers to the antecedent "dogs" and should be translated "puppies."

In the Kition plaque dogs and puppies (or better, their attendants) were thus paid a sum for services rendered, probably in the temples of Mukol or Resheph-Mukol. Thus, this plaque provides an important contemporaneous and complementary document for interpreting the hundreds of dog and puppy burials at Ashkelon.

Although I reiterate that we have thus

far not found an actual temple or any other kind of architecture that can be associated with the dog burials at Ashkelon, I believe there was either a temple or a sacred precinct associated with the cemetery. We may yet find it.

The concentration of dog burials in a cemetery, the type of interment in unlined pits and the mortality profile of the dogs in the Ashkelon cemetery also resemble dog burials in Mesopotamia associated with the goddess of healing, Gula/Ninisina. Her healing cult flourished at several centers during the second and first millennia B.C.

Recently a temple dedicated to the goddess of healing was partially excavated at Nippur, in modern Iraq. A votive figurine of a man clutching his throat has been interpreted by the excavator, Professor MacGuire Gibson of the University of Chicago, as signifying the ailment of which the suppliant either hoped to be or was healed.[12] In cuneiform texts the temple of this goddess of healing (Gula) is sometimes referred to as the "Dog House" (É-ur-gi₇-ra), and her emblem is the dog.[13]

At Isin, another site in Mesopotamia, about 20 miles south of Nippur, numerous votive plaques and figurines depicting dogs were found in another temple of the healing goddess Gula. But even more revealing for our purposes were the 33 dog burials found in the ramp leading up to the temple. They, like the Ashkelon dogs, were buried in shallow pit graves, the carcass then being covered with soil.

Although the sample of dogs excavated at Isin is quite small in comparison with Ashkelon, nevertheless, the mortality profile of the two dog populations is similar: At Isin, puppies comprised nearly half (15 of 33) of the dog burials; the rest were adults and subadults. Like the dogs at Ashkelon, there were no signs that the Isin dogs had died of anything other than natural causes. Again like the dogs of Ashkelon, the Isin dogs were given careful burials regardless of age at death.[14] At Isin, however, the dog burials are clearly related to the temple of Gula, the goddess of healing. They were once the dogs of Gula, the goddess of healing. They roamed about the sacred precincts and participated in the healing rituals. The dogs buried at Ashkelon probably did the same thing.—L.E.S.

[1] See, for example, Nina Jidejian, *The Story of Lebanon in Pictures* (Araya, Lebanon: Imprimerie Catholique, 1985), pp. 150-151.
[2] *Corpus Inscriptionum Semiticarum* (CIS) 86.
[3] CIS 89-90.
[4] H. Donner and W. Röllig, *Kanaanäische und Aramäische Inschriften*, 34 (Weisbaden: Harrassowitz).
[5] W.F. Albright, *Yahweh and the Gods of Canaan* (Garden City, NY: Doubleday, 1968), pp. 148-150.
[6] CIS I.10. In Job 6:4, Job laments that the "arrows of the Almighty" are in him and that he "drinks their poison." Just before, Resheph appears in rather thin disguise—when Job's friend Eliphaz says, "Man is born to trouble as surely as the 'sons of Resheph' [usually translated 'sparks' or 'birds'] fly upward" (Job 5:7). That firebrands were meant seems likely from Psalm 76:4 (English 76:3), where God "breaks the burning arrows (rišpe-qešet), the shield, the sword and the weapons of

war." And in Habakkuk 3:5, Yahweh the Divine Warrior marches forth with two angels of death in his vanguard: "Before him Pestilence (Deber) marched. Plague (Resheph) went forth at his feet." See William F. Albright, *Yahweh and the Gods*, p. 186; Frank Moore Cross, *Canaanite Myth and Hebrew Epic* (Cambridge, MA: Harvard Univ. Press, 1973), pp. 102-103.
[7] William J. Fulco, *The Canaanite God Rešep* (New Haven, CT: American Oriental Society, 1976), pp. 49-54; Walter Burkert, *Greek Religion*, transl. John Raffan (Cambridge, MA: Harvard Univ. Press, 1985), pp. 145-147. See also his *Homo Necans: The Anthropology of Ancient Greek Sacrificial Ritual and Myth*, transl. Peter Bing (Berkeley, CA: Univ. of California Press, 1983), p. 39, note 19. For survival of older cults in Hellenistic-Roman Palestine, including that of Resheph-Mukol, see David Flusser, "Paganism in Palestine," in *The Jewish People in the First Century*, ed. S. Safrai and M. Stern (Philadelphia: Fortress, 1976), vol. 2, p. 1070.
[8] James Pritchard, *The Ancient Near East in Pictures* (Princeton, NJ: Princeton Univ. Press, 2nd ed., 1969), no. 487.
[9] Howard Clark Kee, *Miracle in the Early Christian World* (New Haven, CT: Yale Univ. Press, 1983), p. 85
[10] A. Van den Branden, "Notes pheniciennes," *Bulletin du Musée de Beyrouth* 13 (1956), pp. 92-95; "Elenco delle spese del tempio di Cition, CIS. 86A e B," *Bibliotheca Orientalis* 8 (1966), pp. 257-259.
[11] For an excellent analysis of this difficult text, see Brian Peckham, "Notes on a Fifth-Century Phoenician Inscription from Kition, Cyprus (CIS 86)," *Orientalia* 37 (1968), pp. 304-324, and especially p. 317 for a critique of the identification of klbm and grm with cultic prostitutes.
[12] McGuire Gibson, "Nippur, 1990: The Temple of Gula and a Glimpse of Things to Come," *Oriental Institute Annual Report* (Chicago: Oriental Inst. Press, 1990), pp. 17-26.
[13] A. Livingstone, "The Isin 'Dog House' Revisited," *Journal of Cuneiform Studies* 40 (1988), pp. 54-60.
[14] J. Boessneck, "Die Hundeskellete von Isan Bahriyat (Isin) aus der Zeit um 1000 v. Chr.," in B. Hrouda, et al. (eds.) *Isin—Išan Bahrīyāt I: Die Ergebnisse der Ausgrabungen 1973-1974* (Munich: Bayerische Akademie der Wissenschaften, 1977), pp. 97-109.

(continued from p. 33)

their hair and weigh it against silver or gold, and then give the money to the attendants of the animals mentioned [including dogs]."[10] According to the Kition plaque, discussed in the box on the previous page, it was the attendants who were paid for the services involving healing rites performed by the sacred "dogs and puppies" in the Phoenician temple at Kition.

This is also the context in which we should understand the Deuteronomist's condemnation of those who bring the "wages of a dog into the house of Yahweh in payment for any vow" (Deuteronomy 23:18). There were probably healing cults involving sacred dogs operating in the vicinity of the Jerusalem Temple. It is in such a cultic context that I would—at least tentatively—understand the hundreds of puppy and dog burials at Ashkelon. We do not know the name of the deity with whom these sacred dogs were associated (Resheph-Mukol or Eshmun [= Asklepios]?—see the box pp. 34-36) nor do we yet have the temple to which the dogs might have belonged. Until the temple or other cultic architecture is found, our hypothesis must be regarded as unconfirmed.

If anyone has a better explanation for the immense dog cemetery at Ashkelon, I would like to hear it. ◙

[1] Pseudo-Scylax, Periplus; see Menachem Stern, *Greek and Latin Authors on Jews and Judaism* (Jerusalem: Israel Academy of Sciences and Humanities, 1984), vol. 3, p. 10.
[2] Pompeius Trogus-Justin, Book XIX.i.10.
[3] *Greek Anthology*, transl. W.R. Patton, Loeb Classical Library (New York: G. P. Putnam's Sons, 1917), vol. 2, p. 117, poem 211.
[4] Personal communication from Professor Amihai Mazar.
[5] Mary Boyce, *Zoroastrians: Their Religious Beliefs and Practices* (London: Routledge and Kegan Paul, 1984), pp. 45ff.
[6] Personal communication from Professor Richard Frye.
[7] After the original carvings on both sides of the ivory comb were made, the edges of the comb were, for some unknown reason, pared off. Dr. Abbas Alizadeh, associate director of the Leon Levy expedition, has restored the motifs on the basis of contemporary parallels from ancient Persia in the drawings which he produced. Dr. A. Eran, staff metrologist, identified the weight as one *karsha*, a Persian unit equal to 10 shekels.
[8] Diodorus Siculus, *Bibliotheca historia* (Library of History), transl. C.H. Oldfather, Loeb Classical Library (Cambridge, MA: Harvard Univ. Press, 1933), Book I.83.2; 84.5; 83.5-6.
[9] For a general survey of ancient Near Eastern and Mediterranean healing deities, such as Gula and Asklepios, see Hector Avalos, "Illness and Health Care in Ancient Israel: A Comparative Study of the Role of the Temple (Ph.D. dissertation, Harvard University, Cambridge, MA, 1991), chs. 1-2. Dr. Avalos translated the neo-Assyrian text.
[10] Diodorus, Bk. I.83.2.

EROTICISM & INF

Throughout most of its 5,000-year history, Ashkelon's fortunes and destiny were tied to the sea. As a major Mediterranean seaport, it was a commercial and cultural center. From the highlands to the east, a cornucopia of produce and products flowed down to its warehouses before shipment to other ports around the Mediterranean. Olive oil, wine, timber, resin, meat, hides, wool, limestone and chalk, handicrafts and textiles were some of the commodities from the hinterland. The nearby plains and major valleys were breadbaskets for wheat, some of which was also exported through Ashkelon. From the immediate vicinity of the city, fish, wine, garden crops and textiles were, in different periods, part of the local export.

In return special wines, oils, perfumes, pottery, precious metals, such as silver and especially gold, were imported from distant lands. Some of these imported items were then exchanged farther inland. No doubt much of the profit that accrued from this international exchange went into the coffers of the big-time import-export merchants of Ashkelon, who sat astride the major sea-lanes and overland routes and who were the only ones really to know the price differentials between the point of production and the point of final sale at some faraway port. This oligarchy of merchants exercised economic power through the knowledge of supply and demand

Preceding pages: *Draped in pantaloons and turbans, a group of 19th-century Ashkelonites socialize in the foreground; the remains of the city's former grandeur lie in the distance. The scene, which shows remains no longer extant, was captured in 1839 by Scottish artist David Roberts and is one of a series of hand-painted lithographs he published in 1855 based on a tour of the Holy Land.*

A modern-day artist, using the results of current excavations as well as this depiction by Roberts, has rendered this scene as it might have appeared about the beginning of the early third century A.D. (inset). In the foreground stood a building, possibly a Roman temple, based solely on Roberts—it has not been uncovered in the current excavations nor is it mentioned in classical sources. At center stood a third-century A.D. basilica discovered in 1815 by Lady Hester Lucy Stanhope, Ashkelon's first excavator. Buried beyond the basilica and at a right angle to it lay the remains of another building, misidentified by British archaeologist John Garstang in the 1920s as King Herod's peristyle (colonnades, or cloister) and Senate Hall (bouleuterion). Author Lawrence E. Stager contends that the latter building is in fact another third-century A.D. basilica, or forum.

Other remains shown here and discussed by Stager are a Roman-period theater (seen as a series of concentric circles beyond and slightly to the right of Stanhope's basilica; see photo, opposite, bottom) and the remnants of Fatimid (10th-12th centuries A.D.) fortification walls that cap the heights in the background.

and gave definition to what was real "port power."

Throughout its history as a seaport, Ashkelon was also a center for intellectual exchange, for the flow of ideas and for the intermingling of different customs and of a variety of languages.

In addition to providing commercial and intellectual exchange, seaports also provided a center for the transmission of disease. Ships carried plagues and epidemics along with their precious cargoes. The sailor's delight—wine, women and song—promoted and encouraged the spread of social diseases as well. It is not so surprising to find healing cults, such as we associated with deities and dogs in Part II, located at portside in fifth-century B.C. harbor towns like Ashkelon and like Kition on Cyprus. As we have already seen, a succession of peoples and cultures dominated life in Ashkelon throughout the Bronze and Iron Ages—the Canaanites, followed by the Philistines, and then by the Phoenicians. Foreign merchants, some perhaps living in mercantile enclaves or quarters within the city, added to the variety. In Part III, we will examine the effects of Hellenization on local cultures, the persistence of older customs and ideas along with the introduction of new ones. Then we will examine the relationships of Greco-Romans (pagans), Jews, Christians and Moslems, as powerful new ideas and ideologies vie for the soul of ancient Ashkelon during its last 1,000 years.

By 147 B.C., the Jews, under the leadership of Judas Maccabeus and his brothers, successfully revolted against their Syrian overlords, the Seleucids, and established a line of succession known as the Hasmonean dynasty. But the war had not yet ended. Apollonius, the Seleucid governor, led a powerful army encamped near the Mediterranean coast not far from the old territory of Philistia. Jonathan, one of the Maccabean brothers who by then not only was the secular leader of the new Jewish nation (the Second Commonwealth) but had also taken the title of high priest, led a force of thousands to challenge Apollonius' army on the coastal plain. When Jonathan's forces routed the Seleucid forces, Apollonius' men fled to the old Philistine town of Ashdod, then known as Azotus. Jonathan pursued them; he "burned and plundered Azotus with its neighboring towns, and destroyed by fire both the temple of Dagon [the old Philistine god] and the men who had taken refuge in it" (1 Maccabees 10:84).

To avert a similar disaster, the people of nearby Ashkelon "came out to meet [Jonathan] with great pomp." Ashkelon thus escaped destruction. Jonathan and his army then returned to Jerusalem "laden with much booty," some of which came from Ashkelon (1 Maccabees 10:86-87; see also 1 Maccabees 11:60).

Ashkelon had a knack for maintaining its autonomy. True, when Alexander the Great conquered the Levant in about 332 B.C., Ashkelon, like most of the then-known world, became part of his empire. On Alexander's death in 323 B.C., his empire split in two—the Seleucids of Syria in the north and the Ptolemies of Egypt in the south claiming different parts of it. The Ptolemies ruled Ashkelon until 198 B.C. Then it was the Seleucids' turn. But throughout the Maccabean period (152-37 B.C.), Ashkelon retained its autonomy. Indeed, Ashkelon was able to maintain its autonomy throughout the Roman period (37 B.C.-324 A.D.) as well.

From about 375 B.C. to 235 A.D., Ashkelon issued coins almost continuously (see p. 46 for examples). Bronze and silver coins were minted there during both Ptolemaic and Seleucid rule. During the first century B.C., Ashkelon minted its own silver shekels.

Culturally, like the other cities along the Mediterranean coast, Ashkelon underwent a process of Hellenization in which Greek language, conventions and institutions prevailed. The effects of Alexander's conquest were long-lasting and essentially irreversible. Yet, despite the Hellenistic overlay, the older substratum of Phoenician culture that we described in Part II was never totally eradicated.

In the first century B.C., Ashkelon's silver shekels bore the dove, symbol of Tyche-Astarte (the Greco-Roman and Phoenician goddess) and symbol of the autonomous city mint. The inscription was in Greek. It read: "Of the people of Ascalon, holy, city of asylum, autonomous."[1]

Ashkelon not only had the most active mint in Palestine; the city was also an important banking center. We even know the name of one of its prominent bank-

A mercantile crossroad. *Ashkelon's port and its strategic location along the Mediterranean coast made the city a hub of international trade. The finds shown here came from a plastered cistern dating to the second century B.C. Clockwise from the top in the photo at right is an amphora with a stamped handle to hold wine, from the island of Rhodes; a locally made amphoriskos (small amphora); a small ceramic bottle, known in Latin as an unguentarium, for holding perfumed oils; a decorated item, perhaps used to fill lamps with oil; a carinated bowl with folded horizontal handles, partially decorated with black slip; a Black Glaze bowl with a rosette at center, imported from Italy; and a local red slip jug.*

ers, a certain Philostratus.[2]

As we have already noted, for much of its history, Ashkelon's prosperity was based mainly on its importance as a seaport. The famous Letter of Aristeas* (c. 150 B.C.) mentions Ashkelon along with Joppa, Gaza and Ptolemais (Acco) as Mediterranean harbors "well placed to serve trade."[3] That Ashkelon was a great emporium of commodities as well as a center of exchange during the entire Greco-Roman era is nicely illustrated in a cistern we excavated in the basement of what had once been an impressive villa (Grid 38 [upper]). The cistern went out of use sometime in the last half of the second century B.C. The discarded tableware found in the cistern included fine ceramic imports from Greece and the island of Chios. Also discarded in the cistern when the villa was abandoned were transport amphorae, which were once filled with wines from Rhodes and Italy.

Ashkelon was not only an emporium of commodities, it was also an emporium of ideas. One of its sons, a certain Antiochus (born in about 125 B.C.), became head of the prestigious philosophical Academy in Athens, where he tried to reconcile the philosophies of Plato, Aristotle and the Stoics.[4] Other philosophers, rhetoricians, orators and grammarians taught in the schools of Ashkelon and Gaza. Dorotheus of Ashkelon compiled a lexicon of Attic Greek. Several Ashkelonites were honored abroad in Italy and Greece, as we know from inscriptions found in such distant places as Naples, Puteoli, Athens and Delos.[5]

Herod the Great displaced the Hasmonean dynasty of Judea in 37 B.C. He ruled until 4 B.C., but the so-called Herodian period lasted until 70 A.D. when the Romans destroyed Jerusalem. According to one tradition, Herod was born in Ashkelon; his grandfather is said

---

* The so-called Letter of Aristeas is really a lengthy discourse in the tradition of Hellenistic literature. The author Aristeas (probably a pseudonym) provides the classic view concerning how the Torah (or the Pentateuch) was translated from Hebrew into Greek in just 72 days by 72 elders brought to Alexandria at the behest of Ptolemy Philadelphus (283-246 B.C.); this translation of the first five books of the Hebrew Bible was called the Septuagint (LXX), but the term was later extended to include all of the Hebrew Bible translated at various times into Greek. See Leonard J. Greenspoon, "Mission to Alexandria: Truth and Legend About the Creation of the Septuagint, the First Bible Translation," *Bible Review*, August 1989.

The spirits of thespians past *linger over the site shown in this aerial photo. Despite its classical appearance, the structure is a modern-day theater; excavators believe that ancient Ashkelonites enjoyed theatrical performances on this very spot, in the city's Roman-period theater. The site is the only tiered crater in the vicinity and the sole remnant of the ancient theater, a marble seat, was found nearby.*

Before the modern theater was built, Christian and Islamic legend referred to the stepped depression as the Wells of Abraham. Author Stager points out that this pious belief could have had a basis in fact—involving water, but probably not Abraham. The theater probably had a parados, or fountain, fed by a nearby spring or well, to freshen the air and to keep the spectators away from the stage.

Ironically, the modern theater was host for several years to regional dog shows. Perhaps the spirits of the many canines that once inhabited Ashkelon (see Part II about Ashkelon's unusual dog cemetery), like those of the departed actors, continued to haunt this lovely coastal city.

to have been a servant in the temple of Apollo at Ashkelon.[6]

When Herod became king, he bestowed great honors upon his birthplace by building "baths and ornate fountains for the population of Ascalon, with colonnades [Greek, *peristula*] remarkable for their workmanship and size."[7] Herod also built a palace in Ashkelon for Emperor Augustus. Upon Herod's death, Augustus bestowed it upon Herod's sister, Salome.[8]

The British archaeologist John Garstang, who excavated at Ashkelon in the 1920s, thought he had found Herod's colonnades (Garstang called it the peristyle-colonnades, or cloisters) adjoining what Garstang called the *bouleuterion*, or Senate Hall (located in Grids 40 and 47). We consider these to be a single building; because we date it to the second or third century A.D., however, we will consider this building a bit later.

In the southeast corner of the city is a puzzling circular depression. According to tradition, which persisted among Arabs into the 20th century, this circular depression is Bir Ibrahim, or the Wells of Abraham (also called the Well of Abraham). As our staff geologist and polymath, Professor Frank Koucky of Wooster College, was the first to observe, this circular depression is stepped. It is in fact the impression of an ancient theater. The steps indicate where tiers of marble seats were once set. Not far from the theater, Koucky located an upended, carved block of marble, which looked very much like an ancient theater seat as it lay there on the green grass of one of the picnic grounds in what is now Ashkelon's park. It confirmed Koucky's suggestion that the circular depression was indeed the remains of a theater.

This lonely theater seat and the tiered crater were all that remained of the ancient theater. The rest of the theater seats, like so much other fine quarried masonry (especially marble) exposed at Ashkelon, had been robbed out, or "recycled," for use in other buildings; for centuries after Ashkelon's major destruction in 1191 A.D. and its final destruction in 1270 A.D.— continuing into modern times—boats, barges and even trucks have been hauling away the finest masonry of the ruins for construction elsewhere. Only recently, since the site has been protected by antiquity laws, has the looting been curtailed.

The theater had originally been quarried out of bed-

A theater ticket *for an unknown play. The Ashkelon skyline (as on the mosaics opposite) decorates one side of a lathe-carved bone token (top). The token measures a little more than an inch in diameter. The other side has a Greek word (Phamolēs) in the middle, perhaps the name of a prominent local family, the Roman numeral VIII at the top and the Greek letter eta (H, which also has the value of eight) below. The letter and number may designate the section of Ashkelon's theater reserved for this particular family.*

rock—local sandstone. Usually this style of construction is considered Greek rather than Roman. Roman theaters were most often built above ground level on a series of foundation vaults. However, one small find indicates that this was indeed a Roman-period theater of the first or second century A.D. In our excavations, we found a small bone token that was an ancient theater ticket. Carved on one side is a Greek inscription, "*Phamoles*," with the Roman numeral VIII above the name and the Greek letter *eta* (H) below. *Phamolēs* may be the name of a prominent Ashkelon family; the Roman numeral and Greek letter may indicate the section of the orchestra reserved for members of this family. On the other side of this theater ticket are carved some multistoried buildings. This seems to have been the architectural logo of the city. On two famous mosaics—the Madaba map and the floor of Umm er-Rasas, both in Jordan— Ashkelon is represented by multistoried buildings.

Apparently unaware of the past usage of this circular depression, modern Ashkelonites have erected a theater—much smaller than the ancient one—in the very crater where its Greco-Roman predecessor once stood.

But what of the Arab tradition that this depression is what is left of the Wells of Abraham? Actually, the tradition is also preserved in early Christian sources. The earliest Arab record of the tradition is by the 14th-century writer Ibn Batutah. But long before then, the renowned Wells of Abraham were mentioned by the early Church Fathers Eusebius of Caesarea (260-340 A.D.) and Origen (185/186-254/255 A.D.). The wells were believed to have been dug by the Patriarch himself. As early as the fourth century A.D., Ashkelon was one of the ports of call where Christian pilgrims disembarked. One of the first sites they would have visited was the famous Wells of Abraham. According to Origen, the wells had a "strange and extraordinary style of construction."[9] One of Origen's contemporaries, Eustathius of Antioch, took Origen to task for his allegorical interpretation of the wells.[10] But perhaps Origen's description of the wells was more accurate than either Eustathius or modern scholars have given him credit for. If there had once been a theater in the hollow, it probably had a *parados*, or fountain, with water channels that freshened the air of the theater and separated the spectators from the

actors. By the fourth century all that remained was a theater in ruins in which a spring (or well) still flowed.[11]

One of the impressive buildings second- and third-century visitors to Ashkelon would have seen was the building Garstang misidentified as a combination of King Herod's peristyle (colonnades, or cloister) and the apsidal Senate Hall (*bouleuterion*). It was over 350 feet long and about 115 feet wide (see artist's rendition on the next page). In the center was an open, rectangular courtyard, surrounded by a portico with 24 columns on a side. The columns once stood over 25 feet high, including the Corinthian capitals. The columns, sculpture and wall-facing were made of imported marble. On the south side of the building was an apse, over 40

Ashkelon in stone. *Two mosaics show Ashkelon as it appeared during the Byzantine period. At left, with the name ASKALO[N] in capital letters, is a detail of the sixth-century A.D. Madaba map from a church in Madaba, Jordan, showing what may have been Ashkelon's Eastern, or Jerusalem, Gate at upper right. Buildings are depicted near the city wall at upper left; the colonnaded decumanus, or main east-west street, leads down from the gate to a plaza and to what may have been a Roman-period triumphal arch. The mosaic below is from the eighth-century A.D. Church of St. Stephen at Umm er-Rasas, also in Jordan. A multistoried edifice flanks a columned, rotundalike structure, above which the name ASKALON appears.*

Ashkelon's multistoried buildings, as seen on these mosaics and on the theater ticket opposite, apparently served as symbols of the city—a kind of municipal logo.

Commerce, government and recreation *often intermingled in the public buildings of the Roman world. An artist recreates the environment in a huge basilica at Ashkelon, located just beyond and at a right angle to Lady Hester Stanhope's basilica.*

The impressive building reconstructed here, based on extant remains and on other basilicas from the period, was more than 350 feet long and 115 feet wide. Twenty-five-foot-high columns, topped with Corinthian capitals, bordered a rectangular open courtyard. The two niches on either side of the far doorway held statues of Nike, goddess of Victory (below). Giving a further air of opulence to the structure was the imported marble used for the columns, sculpture and wall-facing.

John Garstang, who uncovered this structure in the 1920s, thought this was Herod's peristyle (colonnades, or cloister) and Senate Hall (bouleuterion), but the building's capitals, reliefs and inscriptions all point to a date during the Severan dynasty (late-second to early-third centuries A.D.). Accordingly, author Stager refers to it as a Severan basilica, an architectural term that does not imply a religious function (though churches from the fourth century on frequently adopted the basilica style).

ANDREW HERSCHER

ILAN SZTULMAN

Nike, Greek goddess of Victory, *winged but headless (left), stands atop a globe shouldered by Atlas, the mythological hero who supports the world. She holds a wreath and a palm. This and an almost identical second statue of Nike flanked a doorway in the public building depicted above.*

Another Greek deity, a crouching Aphrodite (right), goddess of love, beauty and fertility, also once filled a wall niche in this basilica.

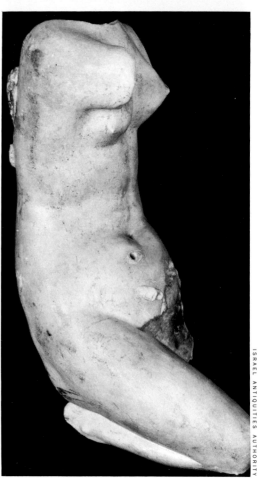

ISRAEL ANTIQUITIES AUTHORITY

feet in diameter, flanked on both sides by square rooms. Greek inscriptions found nearby mention two Roman citizens, Aulus Iustulius Tances, a centurion of the Tenth Legion, and Tiberius Julius Micio, a citizen of Ashkelon; both were honored by the council (*boulē*) and the people (*demos*) of Ashkelon. On the basis of the style of the capitals, the reliefs and other inscriptions, the late Professor Michael Avi-Yonah of the Hebrew University in Jerusalem dated the building to the late second or early third century A.D.

Several marbles found by Garstang—a small white marble statue of a "Crouching Aphrodite" about a foot and a half high (see photo opposite, bottom right); a marble pillar carved in relief depicting the Egyptian goddess Isis flanked by the infant Horus; and two marble pillars depicting Victoria-Nike, goddess of Victory, holding a wreath and a palm and standing full-front on a globe supported on the shoulders of Atlas (see photo opposite, left)—have all been identified by Professor Cornelius Vermeule of Boston College and the Boston Museum of Fine Arts as part of a contemporary program of decoration executed during the Severan dynasty, most likely in the first decade of the third century A.D.[12]

Another equally impressive basilica at Ashkelon was exposed by Lady Hester Stanhope in 1815. She was looking for a treasure hidden at Ashkelon and marked on an Italian monk's map that had come to her attention. During her treasure hunt she uncovered the basilica as well as a statue of a cuirassed soldier. In order to prove to the Ottoman sultan that she had no interest in taking antiquities home to England, she ordered the statue smashed. Most early commentators assumed that she destroyed the statue in the hope of finding the treasure of Ashkelon buried therein, but this was not the case.* Fortunately, her personal physician, Dr. Charles Lewis Meryon, who traveled with her, made a sketch of the cuirassed statue before it was smashed. His sketch is sufficient to date the statue and the basilica to the Severan period as well.[13]

After redating the sculpture and the two monumental peristyle buildings (discovered by Stanhope and by Garstang) to the Severan period, I could then see that the organization of Roman Ashkelon bore a striking resemblance to the New Forum, with its civic center and marketplace, which the emperor Septimius Severus (193-211 A.D.) built along the harbor of his birthplace Lepcis (or Leptis) Magna in Tripolitania, North Africa.

Adjacent to the area where Lady Hester Stanhope's basilica was located, we excavated a villa in Grid 38 (upper) that was part of a distinctly patrician neighborhood. The villa had a marvelous view to the north, overlooking terraced gardens and the large basilica exposed by Lady Hester. In a small room on the north side of the villa, we found hundreds of eggshell-thin sherds that had once been discs of ceramic oil lamps. Some of the larger fragments bore erotic motifs, others had mythological motifs (see photos on p. 47).

The lamps had all been made in molds. None of them had ever been lit; although a terra-cotta bull and a kneeling ceramic camel laden with amphorae were available to fill the lamps with olive oil, there were no soot marks on any of them from burnt wicks. So it is unlikely they were ever used. When the lamps are pieced together perhaps the purpose of the roomful of lamps will become clearer. The room where they were found does front on a small street, but it seems unlikely that oil lamps were being sold from the ground floor of such a patrician villa. Our best guess at the moment is that this collection of erotic and mythological lamps and other notions found in the room was solely for the amusement of the owner.

Lest the reader conclude that the inhabitants of Ashkelon were unusually lascivious, it should be pointed out that similar erotic lamps have been found in every major city in Palestine as well as elsewhere in the empire during the Roman period. Even in Jerusalem, whose name was changed by the Romans in the second century A.D. to Aelia Capitolina, numerous erotic lamps have been uncovered in the excavations led by Professor Benjamin Mazar adjacent to the Temple Mount.[14]

Based on the distribution of erotic lamps throughout the Roman world, we conclude that the erotic lamps from Ashkelon probably belonged to a Greco-Roman household, rather than to a Jewish or a Christian household. The Romans no doubt thought the lamps sexually titillating and perhaps even arousing.

Roman attitudes toward human sexuality contrasted sharply with contemporaneous Jewish and Christian attitudes, so much so that the presence of lamps depicting both heterosexual and homosexual scenes would have been quite incongruous in a Jewish or a Christian home.

In Roman families, the ideal daughter was expected to enter marriage a virgin and then to remain faithful to her husband throughout marriage. However, a double standard was applied to males. Little or no stigma was attached to sexual affairs before or during marriage, whether with males or females. For freeborn males, premarital and extramarital affairs were socially acceptable so long as they did not violate norms pertaining to power and status in Roman society. It was socially acceptable, for example, for young bachelors, or a married man and a young bachelor, to have sex together. Sexual relations with a person of inferior status, such as a slave or a foreigner or a prostitute, regardless of gender, fell within the boundaries of acceptable behavior. Adultery, involving the wife of another freeborn Roman, did not. Fleeting liaisons, however, should remain discreet and not be confused with much more serious marital relationships.

The dominant status of the Roman male was also expressed in his domineering role in sexual relationships. Sodomy and, to a lesser extent, pederasty were acceptable behavior—as we see from one of the lamps—so long as the older, higher-born male played the active role of sodomist, not catamite. Because of his dominant status and power, it was considered a gross violation of the moral order for a Roman male to per-

* See Neil A. Silberman, "Restoring the Reputation of Lady Hester Lucy Stanhope," **BAR**, July/August 1984.

Fort Knox on the Mediterranean.
Ashkelon minted coins for a nearly unbroken 600-year span, from about 375 B.C. to 235 A.D.

These three second- and third-century A.D. coins—shown with the obverse and reverse side by side—testify not only to the city's wealth as a seaport but also to the staying power of Phoenician culture even into the Roman period.

The coin above bears the portrait of Septimius Severus, Roman emperor from 193-211 A.D. Its reverse side

(top, right and a drawing below it from a similar coin) depicts a series of doorways leading to the inner sanctum of the temple of Phanēbalos at Ashkelon. Phanēbalos is the Greek transcription of panē Ba'al (Face of Ba'al), a common name for Tanit, the Phoenician goddess whose consort was the mountain god Ba'al Ḥamōn. The outer doorway shown here is flanked by columns supporting a disc and crescent (symbol of either Tanit or Ba'al Ḥamōn), with a frieze of Egyptian cobras above the lintel.

The two other coins shown here portray Phanēbalos/Tanit herself. On the reverse side of both coins, Tanit raises her right arm brandishing a sword and holds a shield and a palm branch on her left arm. The obverse sides of these coins feature a profile of Julia Domna, second wife of Septimius Severus, and, at bottom, Elagabalus, Roman emperor from 218 to 222 A.D.

form fellatio or cunnilingus on his sexual partner—just as it was against nature for a woman to behave like a man, or to mount her lover.

By contrast, contemporaneous Jews and Christians adhered to what we would consider a much stricter sexual code, based on Biblical injunctions. Both groups condemned adultery and homosexuality (see, for example, Exodus 20:14; Leviticus 18:22, 20:13; 1 Corinthians 6:9; Romans 1:26-27, 2:22; 1 Timothy 1:10). Fidelity was the key virtue for both husband and wife, without exception. For many Christians in the later Roman period, celibacy was considered the highest form of devotion to God, surpassing even marriage as a virtue, just as it was for St. Paul (although his celibacy should be understood in the context of his expectation of the imminent Parousia, the second coming of Christ at the end-time).

For married couples, both Jewish and Christian, sex was for procreation, not recreation. "Be fruitful and multiply" was the divine blessing (Genesis 1:28). Jews and Christians took a pro-natalist attitude toward conception and children. This attitude must have contributed significantly to prohibitions against homosexual and bisexual behavior. They were adamantly against abortion and infanticide, whereas the Romans were not, as we shall soon see in the case of infanticide at Ashkelon in the Byzantine period.[15]

As noted earlier, beneath the heavy veneer of Hellenization and Romanization of Ashkelon, many aspects of the older Oriental culture of the Phoenicians managed to survive. Some of the older religious cults not only survived but actually flourished, especially when they could contribute to, or be incorporated into, the Roman imperial cult. No better example of this phenomenon can be found than the cult of the Phoenician goddess Tanit (mother goddess and virgin bride, consort of Ba'al Hamōn). Tanit was very much a part of the religious life of Ashkelon—and even of Rome—in the third century A.D.

Tanit appears together with Roman emperors and empresses on second- and third-century A.D. coins minted in Ashkelon. Tanit is depicted as a war goddess, brandishing a sword and carrying a shield as well as a palm branch. She is identified in Greek as Phanēbalos; this is a transparent Greek transcription of panē Ba'al, or "Face of Ba'al," a favorite epithet in the Phoenician and Punic languages for Tanit, known from hundreds of inscriptions found at Phoenician Carthage.[16]

The iconography on these Phanēbalos coins suggests that during the Roman period Tanit still had an impressive temple in Ashkelon. Several coins, minted exclusively in Ashkelon, bear a simple temple facade on one side. One, however, depicts an elaborate temple facade rendered in Egypto-Phoenician style.[17] Among the imperial portraits on the Ashkelon coins with Tanit are Emperor Antoninus Pius (who reigned 138-161 A.D.) and Empress Julia Domna, the second wife of Emperor Septimius Severus (who reigned 193-211 A.D.) and a great-aunt of the young Emperor Elagabalus (203-222), who came from the same priestly family as Julia Domna, a priestly line devoted to the cult of Elagabal

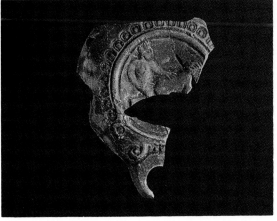

Mythological and heroic characters *(above) decorate two oil lamps from Ashkelon. At top, a charioteer urges on his steeds; Europa and the bull are shown below (according to the myth, Zeus transformed himself into a bull, swam to the seashore where his beloved Europa was playing and carried her off to Crete).*

Found within a villa in a prosperous neighborhood next to the basilica discovered by Lady Hester Stanhope, these and hundreds of other eggshell-thin lamps decorated with mythological and erotic scenes bore no burn marks—an indication that the lamps had not been used or were part of a collection meant only for display.

Erotic activities *(right) appear on the central disc of delicate oil lamps at Ashkelon. Depictions of explicit sexual acts have been found on lamps in every major city of Roman-period Palestine—even in Jerusalem, when it was known as Aelia Capitolina.*

These second- to third-century A.D. lamps reveal much about Greco-Roman attitudes toward sex. Unlike their Jewish or Christian counterparts, Romans saw nothing wrong with homosexual relations or with heterosexual liaisons outside of marriage, provided that the relations comported with their hierarchy of power and status. Thus a freeborn Roman could engage in sex with a social inferior of either sex (such as a slave or a prostitute), but not with the wife of another freeborn Roman.

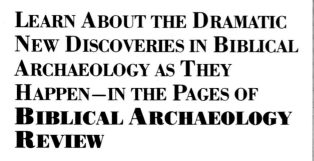

in Emesa, Syria.

At the age of 15, Elagabalus was elevated to emperor. He reigned barely four years. To prepare the Roman senators for this eccentric Syrian ruler, his mother sent ahead a portrait of the handsome youth, bedecked in his sacerdotal robes dyed in Phoenician purple and embroidered with gold thread. But this was not warning enough for what they were about to experience. In a very short time, he managed to create one scandal after another, even in jaded Rome. In addition to being a religious fanatic of the god Elagabal (whom most Romans had probably never heard of before his devotee's arrival), the young emperor was also an exhibitionist—his boyish face, with kohl-darkened eyes and heavily rouged cheeks, peering out from under his jeweled crown. Like many other Roman males, Elagabalus was an ardent bisexual. He frequently made the rounds of the public baths of Rome, sizing up prospective male lovers. Promotions to high office and positions of responsibility were more often made to those who displayed sexual prowess or who granted sexual favors than to those who had competence in governmental matters. His protective mother frequented debates in the Senate and presided over a "female senate," which deliberated about rules of etiquette.[18]

To many Roman senators, the young emperor's effeminate manner must have been disgusting, and a clear violation of the "macho" code for Roman males. His public processions and rituals for the deity Elagabal were no doubt regarded as bizarre. But most intolerable was his political ineptitude, which ultimately led to his (and his mother's) downfall. An aunt orchestrated the murder of both the emperor and his mother, bringing his reign to an end in 222 A.D.

But who was this obscure Syrian deity Elagabal from whom the youthful emperor took his throne name and ultimately his identity? During his brief reign, Elagabalus transported his favorite deity's cult image, a conical "black stone" from Syria, and brought the statue and dowry of the Phoenician goddess Tanit from Carthage. Both were enshrined on the Palatine, and as the divine couple they reigned as the leading deities of Rome. And, of course, therein lies the clue to solving the mystery of the identity of Elagabal; he was none other than Tanit's spouse in Carthage, the well-known Phoenician (and Syrian) deity Ba'al Ḥamōn, or "Lord

An innocent exterior *masked the degenerate character of Elagabalus, emperor of Rome at the precocious age of 15. Having come from Syria, Elagabalus quickly set about establishing the Phoenician/Syrian god Elagabal and the Phoenician goddess Tanit as the leading deities of Rome. His marriage to a Vestal Virgin reenacted the sacred marriage of the divine couple Ba'al Ḥamōn and Tanit. Elagabalus' frequent forays to the public baths in search of male lovers and the subsequent promotions of his sexual partners to high political office soon proved ill-advised. A plot headed by his aunt led to his murder after only four years as emperor.*

of the Mt. Amanus." Actually his Latin name Elagabal disguises another valuable clue to his identity, for it is the latinized form of the Semitic El Jebel, which means "El of the Mountain."[19]

In addition to his forays in the public baths, Emperor Elagabalus married at least four wives during his short reign. One of them was a Vestal Virgin, whom he identified with the goddess Tanit. And, of course, he was Elagabal. Their marriage, then, replicated that of the heavenly couple, Ba'al Ḥamōn (alias Elagabal) and Tanit. Thus these Phoenician deities became part of the imperial cult in Rome. Tanit's temple and cult survived at Ashkelon, and coins bearing her image as Phanēbalos circulated in parts of the Roman world.

Sometime in the fourth century A.D., a bathhouse was built over some earlier Roman villas in Ashkelon, including the villa where we found the erotic lamps. We can't yet decide whether this was a small public bath or a large private one. In any event, it had a much-repaired mosaic floor, so it was used for many years. Finally, in the sixth century A.D., the bath was replaced by a monumental apsidal building.

The bathhouse itself underwent at least one remodeling. In the early phase, the tub was larger. At each corner was a "heart"-shaped column. (Looking down on it, it was shaped like a heart, where two columns had come together at the corner, like this: ▢.) These four columns probably supported a canopy over the plastered tub. In the white mosaic floor was a *tabula ansata* (a rectangle for an inscription with triangles at each end outside the rectangle and pointing toward it, like this: ▷▭◁). The *tabula* was outlined with black tesserae; inside the rectangle was an inscription, but unfortunately it was so badly damaged it could not be read. However, in the next phase, when the tub was smaller, another inscription in Greek, also inside a *tabula ansata*, was written on the outer face of the plaster rim of the tub, just above the spot where the earlier floor inscription had been located. We can surmise that both inscriptions said the same thing. The one on the plastered panel of the tub read in Greek "*eiselthe apolauson kai [.....]*," "Enter, enjoy, and ....."

At first we thought the bath might also have been a brothel. As we saw in the account of the teenage emperor Elagabalus, public baths, then as today, could serve more than one purpose. We later learned, however, that inscriptions like this were not uncommon in

"Enter, enjoy and...." *entices an inscription on a plastered panel on the side of a bathtub inside a fourth- to sixth-century A.D. bathhouse (above). The words lie within a tabula ansata frame—a rectangle with two inward-pointing triangles on either side. Resisting the temptation to plunge in are author Stager (right), director of the Ashkelon excavations, and Douglas Esse, then associate director.*

The bathhouse was built over several earlier villas, including the villa with the erotic lamps. The excavators are not sure whether the upper structure was a small public bath or a large private one. Based on similar inscriptions from other Roman-period bathhouses, the "Enter, enjoy and...." exhortation may have been simply a warm welcome and not a hint of illicit pleasures to be found within.

Graveyard for newborns. *The semicircle at upper right in this bird's-eye view shows the remains of a sixth- to seventh-century A.D. monumental basilica. Excavators do not yet know whether it had a religious or a secular function. Running below it, vertically in the photograph, is a large sewer that was in use at the same time as the bath shown above.*

The sewer contained a grisly find: the remains of nearly 100 infants. Based on their bone size and dental development, the infants were newborns killed very soon after birth. The ancient Greeks and Romans considered infanticide, *especially through abandonment and exposure to the elements, the most effective form of birth control. In this, as with their attitudes towards sexual relations, they differed from their Jewish and Christian counterparts. After Christianity was declared the official religion of the Roman empire, infanticide was banned. The remains at Ashkelon show that the practice continued nonetheless.*

The white area at lower left in the photo is the plastered cistern that contained the second-century B.C. ceramic wares shown on page 41.

bathhouses during the Roman period, and that they did not have sexual connotations.[20] The inscription was simply a warm welcome, whether the bath was public or private.

What was not so warm and friendly was a gruesome discovery in the sewer that ran under the bathhouse. The sewer was large enough for a person to stand up inside it; a gutter ran along its well-plastered bottom. The sewer had been clogged with refuse sometime in the sixth century A.D. When we excavated and dry-sieved the desiccated sewage, we found numerous small bones that we assumed to be animal bones. Only later did we learn from our staff osteologist, Professor Patricia Smith of Hebrew University, that they were human bones—of nearly 100 little babies apparently murdered and thrown into the sewer (see box).

Roman attitudes toward infanticide were quite different from those of Jews and Christians, both of whom, as we noted earlier, were pro-natalist and whose moral teachings forbade the practice. The Greeks and the Romans found infanticide to be the most effective form of birth control.* Abandonment and exposure to the elements and to ravaging animals were the most common method mentioned in classical myths and legends; of course, there was always the possibility that the baby would be rescued and nurtured just as Moses was by the pharaoh's daughter or Romulus and Remus were by the friendly she-wolf.[21] Egyptians, whose religion also forbade infanticide, were allowed to rescue abandoned babies and adopt them as foundlings or rear them as slaves. Greeks and Romans were in the habit of discarding their unwanted infants on manure piles. To memorialize the rescue, Egyptians often gave these babies "copro-" names (such as Kopreus), relating to the dungheap.

Most revealing, though, of the Greco-Roman attitude toward infanticide, is a letter written June 17, 1 B.C., by a certain Hilarion to his pregnant wife, Alis:

"Know that I am still in Alexandria. And do not worry if they all come back and I remain in Alexandria. I ask and beg you to take good care of our baby son, and as soon as I receive payment I will send it up to you. If you are delivered of child [before I get home], if it is a boy keep it, if a girl discard it. You have sent me word, 'Don't forget me.' How can I forget you. I beg you not to worry."[22]

What could be more casual (and callous) than this father's attitude toward the disposal of his newborn daughter?

After Emperor Constantine converted to Christianity and made that the official religion of the empire, a law was put on the books making infanticide illegal. That law, however, failed to deter those fathers and mothers who discarded their newborns in the sewers of Ashkelon. Were most of the helpless victims girls? At the moment physical anthropologists cannot answer that question from skeletal evidence alone. Someday

* See Lawrence E. Stager and Samuel R. Wolff, "Child Sacrifice at Carthage—Religious Rite or Population Control?" **BAR**, January/February 1984.

Bones of a Hundred Infants Found In Ashkelon Sewer

Excavation of the Roman-Byzantine sewer system associated with the bathhouse at Ashkelon revealed the skeletons of nearly 100 infants. They were found mixed in with the garbage more commonly associated with such contexts—broken potsherds, animal bones, murex shells and odd coins. Most of the infant bones were intact, and all parts of the skeleton were represented. Since infant bones are fragile, they tend to fragment when disturbed or moved for secondary burial. The good condition of the infant bones at Ashkelon indicated to us that the infants had been tossed into the drain soon after death with the soft tissues intact. This manner of disposal of the infants indicates a rather callous attitude, suggesting that these might represent abortions or infanticide, rather than death from natural causes.

We focused closely on the age range of the infants as one indication of the cause of death. The rationale for using age range as an indicator of the cause of death is that perinatal death in all populations studied shows a comparable pattern of mortality. There is a high rate of mortality in the first month of life that gradually decreases over the first year, followed by a second peak at weaning. If the drain served as a mass grave following some catastrophe, or was the normal way of disposing of infants who died when young and were not accorded full burial rites, then we should expect some variability in the age of death of the infants in the drain. If on the other hand, these infant skeletons were the result of infanticide practiced immediately after birth, all would be of the same age.

Examination of the Ashkelon sample showed that all the infants were approximately the same size and with the same degree of dental development. Both bone size and dental development were equivalent to that of newborn infants. Moreover, forensic tests showed no neonatal lines in the teeth. These are considered evidence of survival of more than three days after birth. Their absence in the Ashkelon infants reinforces the hypothesis of death at birth.

A sudden increase in the number of deaths which would result in emergency burial measures, such as have been documented following epidemics, warfare or famine, would affect children of all ages. This does not apply to the skeletons found in the Ashkelon sewer, where only newborns were found. Infanticide in the past (as at present) was (and is) usually carried out immediately after birth, before the development of mother-infant bonding. Child sacrifices, on the other hand, were usually made periodically, so that infants of different ages were sacrificed. While it is conceivable that the infants found in the drain were stillborn, their number, age and condition strongly suggest that they were killed and thrown into the drain immediately after birth.

—Patricia Smith and Gila Kahila,
Hebrew University, Jerusalem

soon, I hope, advances in analytical testing of bone material will provide an answer.

Ashkelon was founded on an underground river. About 15 million years ago it flowed aboveground. But later in prehistoric times, sands from what became the Nile Delta washed up and over the coastal plain of Canaan, forming north-south ridges of loosely cemented sandstone, now the local bedrock known as kurkar. These sands buried the river channel, making it an aquifer, or "drainpipe," that carries fresh water to the coastal plain, seeping to the surface at several places. Dozens of wells, some of them quite ancient, tap this underground water source 60 feet or more below today's picnic grounds of the Ashkelon park. In the past, as today, these fresh waters transformed Ashkelon into a veritable oasis and garden spot.

In the Roman period, Ashkelon was famous for its wheat, henna (still used in the Mediterranean as a vegetable dye for hands and hair), dates and onions, which were displayed at international trade fairs in Gaza as well as Ashkelon.[23] Ashkelon even lent its name ("Ascalon" in classical sources) to a special variety of onion (*caepa Ascalonia*) grown there and exported around the Mediterranean to numerous Roman cities.[24] We know this onion today as the scallion (after Ascalon). (Although Ashkelon lent its name to the onion, it *took* its name from the old Northwest Semitic, probably Canaanite, word TQL, meaning "to weigh";

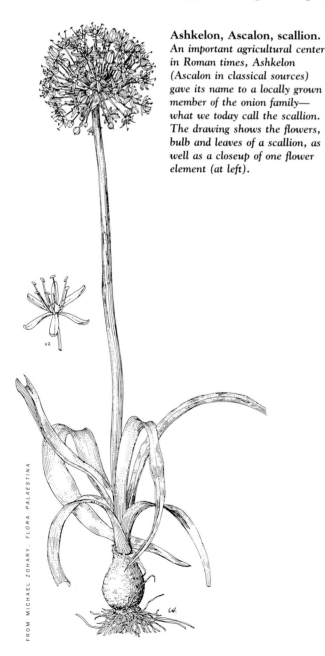

Ashkelon, Ascalon, scallion. *An important agricultural center in Roman times, Ashkelon (Ascalon in classical sources) gave its name to a locally grown member of the onion family— what we today call the scallion. The drawing shows the flowers, bulb and leaves of a scallion, as well as a closeup of one flower element (at left).*

FROM MICHAEL ZOHARY, FLORA PALAESTINA

"shekel" comes from this same root.)

In the fifth to sixth centuries A.D., Ashkelon and Gaza became renowned for their wines.[25] Just how widespread the export of wine from this area was is reflected in the pottery vessels used to transport it. Over 15 years ago, a specialist in Roman pottery, Dr. John Riley, put forth the brilliant hypothesis that a certain type of storage jar—a short and very ugly one he designated Type 2—found at Caesarea actually came from the Gaza region and was "either the container or the forerunner of the container for Gaza wine."[26] This type of amphora is found throughout the Mediterranean and in Europe as far northwest as London. Several exemplars have even been found in Trier (Germany) and in the Crimea. The appearance of these jars in the fourth through sixth centuries A.D. matches precisely the period when Byzantine authors mention wine coming from the Gaza region.

Riley also noted that the highest concentrations of his Type 2 amphora had been found in the Gaza region.

When Riley's exemplars from Caesarea were subjected to petrological analysis, the clay turned out to be from the Gaza area; when compared with a control sample of modern fired clay from Gaza, the clay from the Caesarea amphorae proved to have a similar texture and composition. This confirmed that the Caesarea amphorae had indeed come from the Gaza area.

Our excavations at Ashkelon have now confirmed that these storage jars were used as transport amphorae for exporting local wines.[27] Dr. Barbara Johnson, our staff ceramist and director of the Ashkelon Laboratory in Jerusalem, has studied literally hundreds of thousands of potsherds from the fourth to sixth centuries A.D. recovered in our excavations. A very high percentage of these sherds comes from so-called Gaza-type—perhaps, now, we should add Ashkelon-type—wine jars.

Ashkelon was clearly an important center for the production of these amphorae. In and around construction sites in the modern city of Ashkelon, Frank Koucky has found several kilns in which these ancient vessels had been fired. In addition, in his systematic archaeological survey of the Ashkelon region, Mitchell Allen of UCLA has discovered numerous kilns for producing these amphorae along the sandstone ridges east of the city. Some of these kilns were found in association with wine presses and other buildings, probably components of agricultural estates in the vicinity.[28] The wine presses provide another piece of evidence supporting the suggestion that these transport amphorae should indeed be linked to the wine trade. The coastal region of southern Palestine from south of Gaza north to Ashdod is dotted with manufacturing sites for these storage jars.[29]

This period—the early Byzantine period—was an especially prosperous one in Palestine. Indeed, it was not exceeded until modern times. The population also reached unprecedented heights, unexceeded until the 20th century. Even the desert—east of the southern coastal plain—bloomed, not because of climatic changes, but because of the economic boom. The export of native wines undoubtedly propelled and sustained the boom. Numerous wine presses, some quite large and elaborate, have been found in the Negev desert at cities such as Shivtah, Avdat and Elusa.[30] The demand for these wines was apparently so great that even marginal zones, such as the desert, were worth cultivating by floodwater and runoff techniques of irrigation to produce wine grapes.

Why was there such a demand for wines from Ashkelon, Gaza and elsewhere in Palestine—a demand never equaled before or since? The answer lies, at least in part, in the broader historical picture of the Holy Land in the fourth to sixth centuries A.D.

In 324 A.D. the emperor Constantine officially recognized Christianity. By the late fourth and early fifth centuries A.D., monastic life was flourishing near Gaza and Ashkelon as well as in the Judean Desert. Christianity spread not only into the desert but also in the major cities of Palestine.

Christian pilgrims began to flock to the Holy Land from around the world. From Europe they came in ships that departed regularly from Gaul and Italy, usually sailing via Antioch or Alexandria.

Jerusalem, the holy city, and especially the Holy Sepulchre, were of course primary objectives for these early pilgrims for whom the "testimony of the holy places [was] to substantiate the testimony of the Bible."[31] But they also visited other sacred sites—Bethlehem, Mamre (Hebron), Mt. Sinai (St. Catherine's Monastery) and even Mt. Ararat, where according to the church historian Eusebius "Noah's Ark" was still visible.[32] No doubt they also wanted to see the "Wells of Abraham" at Ashkelon, as mentioned by Origen. For many Western pilgrims, Ashkelon was their first port of call in the Holy Land. Of all the coastal cities south of Jaffa, only Ashkelon actually sits on the seacoast.

These early pilgrims took home with them all sorts of relics and sacred souvenirs—pieces of the Cross, saints' remains, fruit from the "garden of John the Baptist," soil and olive oil used to light lamps at the Holy Sepulchre. The oil was exported in small vials or flasks called *ampullae*; several examples have turned up in our excavations. According to the anonymous sixth-century Pilgrim of Piacenza, who left us his travel notes, the holy oil was sanctified by bringing the flasks in contact with the wood of the Cross, at which time the oil boiled so furiously that the *ampullae* popped their stoppers. These had to be immediately replaced to prevent the precious oil from spilling out.[33]

Like tourists today, pilgrims contributed greatly to the economy of the Holy Land. The relics and souvenirs they brought back must have made a stirring impression on those who could not make, or could not afford, the pilgrimage. There was, however, another commodity, not so easily carried home but apparently also in great demand: wine from the Holy Land, especially wine from the Gaza and Ashkelon regions. It must have been exported in quantity to meet the needs of the churches of Europe. In one sixth-century reference, Gaza wine was bequeathed to a church in Lyons to celebrate the Eucharist.[34]

Ashkelon was an importer as well as an exporter.

CARL ANDREWS

New wine for old amphorae. *Large containers such as this, known as a Gaza wine amphora (or, more technically, as Riley's Type 2 or Killebrew's Type B), carried vast amounts of wine all over the Mediterranean world in the fifth and sixth centuries A.D. Examples have been found as far afield as London, Trier (Germany) and the Crimea.*

Petrological studies of these amphorae show that they were made in the area between Gaza and Ashdod—of which Ashkelon is in the middle. The demand for wine from the Holy Land grew with the sudden increase of pilgrims that followed Constantine's conversion to Christianity in the early fourth century. Pilgrims, as well as those who could not afford the journey, eagerly sought wine from Palestine with which to celebrate the Eucharist. The result was an economic boom for the coastal area; the population grew to a level unmatched until this century and portions of the desert were irrigated by runoff techniques so that they could be cultivated for grape-growing.

Barbara Johnson has identified more than 130 different types of transport amphorae found in our excavations that reached Ashkelon from Spain, Italy, North Africa, Crete, the Aegean and the Black Sea area. This is in addition to more than 30 different types of fine wares, including lovely Cypriot, Italian, African Red Slip, Egyptian and Coptic tablewares.

Thus, the economy boomed as never before. All this a reflection of pilgrimage to the Holy Land—big business, then as now.

In the seventh century A.D. many parts of the Byzantine empire surrendered to the armies of a powerful new religion—Islam. Ashkelon surrendered to the second Caliph of Islam, Omar, in 636, but the Byzantines did not actually evacuate the city until 640. According to the Arab chroniclers, Ashkelon became a beautiful and delightful city once again. Except for pockets of Omayyad pottery in later fills, however, our excava-

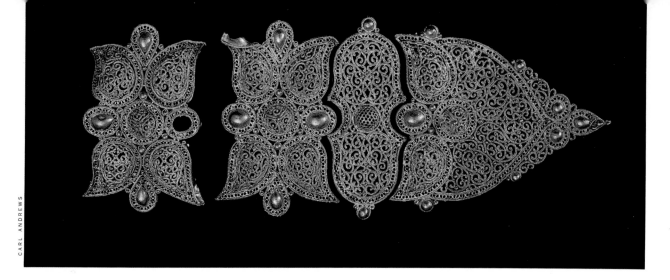

tions have not yet recovered significant remains from this period.

In the Fatimid period (10th-12th centuries A.D.), lovely houses were built along narrow streets; each had a small pool in the courtyard. In the destruction debris and fill next to one of these houses, we recovered four pieces of exquisite 22-karat gold jewelry. Professor Myriam Rosen-Ayalon of the Hebrew University, an expert on Islamic archaeology—and jewelry in particular—found that all four pieces fit together perfectly and belonged to the same larger ensemble; probably the gold pieces were once attached to a soft textile, such as suede or velvet, which was worn as a belt or sash. Each of the four pieces used the same manufacturing technique, combining filigree and granulation, to which gold beads were then added. We marveled at the extraordinary craftsmanship and intricate decorative design—paisley, almond-shaped, S-shaped and heart-shaped motifs.[35]

During the Fatimid period the fortifications of Ashkelon were rebuilt—for the last time on a grand scale.[36] The earliest ramparts had been built by the Canaanites in the Middle Bronze Age II (2000-1550 B.C.). Much of this Canaanite fortification was incorporated into the Fatimid ramparts. Some of the ruined Fatimid ramparts still rise like giant stalagmites around the rim of the last Islamic city. In the Sea Wall rising above the beach, the Fatimids used old Roman columns made of Aswan granite to reinforce their stone and cement masonry. The old Roman columns look like ships' cannons sticking out of the Fatimid wall (see back cover). More Roman columns by the hundreds, if not thousands, lie buried just under the beach sands. They were originally shipped from Egypt to Ashkelon during the Roman period and then reused throughout the next millennium.

In the 12th century A.D., William of Tyre visited Ashkelon and wrote the following vivid description of its defenses:

"[Ashkelon] lies upon the seacoast in the form of a semicircle, the chord or diameter of which extends along the shore while the arc or bow lies on the land looking toward the east. The entire city rests in a

Intricately designed, 22-karat gold *provides a delicate lattice of opulent decoration. This Islamic-period (12th-century A.D.) jewelry was one of a set of four or more that was probably attached to a soft fabric and worn as a sash or belt.*

basin, as it were, sloping to the sea and is surrounded on all sides by artificial mounds, upon which rise the walls with towers at frequent intervals. The whole is built of solid masonry, held together by cement which is harder than stone. The walls are wide, of goodly thickness and proportionate height. The city is furthermore encircled by outworks built with the same solidity and most carefully fortified. There are four gates in the circuit of the wall, strongly defended by lofty and massive towers.

"The first of these, facing east, is called the Greater Gate and sometimes the Gate of Jerusalem, because it faces toward the Holy City. It is surmounted by two very lofty towers which serve as a strong protection for the city below. In the barbican before this gate are three or four smaller gates which one passes to the main entrance by various winding ways. The second gate faces the west. It is called the Sea Gate, because through it people have egress to the sea. The third to the south looks toward the city of Gaza . . . , whence it takes its name. The fourth with outlook toward the north is called the Gate of Jaffa, from the neighbouring city which lies on this same coast."[37]

Ashkelon's Moslem rulers were apparently not as hostile to the two other great monotheistic faiths, Judaism and Christianity, as we might suppose, for we know that Jews continued to reside in Ashkelon throughout the Islamic and Crusader periods. And a Byzantine church, which we excavated in 1985, continued in use throughout most of the medieval period.

During the Crusader period this little church, located just inside and to the south of the Jerusalem Gate, was known as Saint Mary the Green (Santa Maria Viridis).[38]

Originally, in the fifth century, the church was laid out as a basilica, divided into three aisles by two rows of columns made of Aswan granite (imported earlier in the Roman period and reused). The columns supported a gallery and a pitched roof. As we have seen, the basilica plan was used for both secular and sacred architecture during the Roman period at Ashkelon. When

Four granite columns *still stand before the apse of the Santa Maria Viridis—Saint Mary the Green—church. The structure stood from about 400 to about 1191 A.D. A fresco of four saints can still be seen in the apse (see closeup at left). Behind the apse rises masonry from Ashkelon's eastern fortification wall, destroyed in 1191.*

The "Green" in the church's name may be an indication that Saint Mary was considered by the Christians of Ashkelon to be the saint of the city's abundant crops. The term may also refer to a sporting faction, rivals of the Blues throughout the Byzantine world. Charioteers from many localities vied to compete in the "World Championship" races in Constantinople; at these meets sports, religion and politics mixed. A victory by a team was often interpreted as a victory for its city's deity or patron saint. A victory for the Greens of Ashkelon might have been seen as a victory for the Christians and Saint Mary the Green.

Now faded and indistinct, *a fresco of four saints once graced the apse of the Santa Maria Viridis church (above). An artist's rendition (right) shows each reading from Greek scrolls containing excerpts from the sermons of St. John Chrysostom. The fresco dates to about the 12th century.*

the basilica plan was adopted by church architects, the apse was nearly always oriented toward the Holy City, Jerusalem. Thus the apse of our church was located at the east end of the building, next to the city wall. From the apse, water flowed through a lead pipe and settling basin before reaching a marble-lined cruciform baptistry built into the earliest marble floor. The small size and shallowness of the baptistry would indicate that baptism was by sprinkling rather than by immersion.

Santa Maria Viridis continued in use throughout much of the Islamic period until the Fatimids converted it to a mosque in the mid-tenth century. It was restored again as a Byzantine church when the Crusaders conquered Ashkelon. Its plan changed, however: only four of the original six columns were used, suggesting a cruciform vaulted ceiling above the apse. Frescoes were added to the central apse and two side niches. Above the robbed-out bench and bishop's chair (*cathedra*) in the central apse were frescoes of four saints/bishops reading Greek scrolls, each scroll containing excerpts from the homilies of St. John Chrysostom (the "golden-mouthed" bishop of Constantinople, 398-407 A.D.), as recognized immediately by our staff epigraphist for Greek and Latin, Vasilios Tzaferis of the Israel Antiquities Authority.

Santa Maria Viridis attests not only to the continual presence of a community of Byzantine Christians (sometimes referred to as Oriental, or Syrian, Christians) at Ashkelon from the time of its founding—about 400 A.D.—through the Crusader period, but its architectural history reflects in microcosm the fortunes of the Christian and Muslim political and religious empires during eight centuries (c. 400-1200 A.D.) of competition for the soul of Ashkelon and of the world.

The Fatimids dominated Ashkelon until 1153, when the Crusaders conquered the city. Saladin, the great sultan and commander, regained Ashkelon in 1187. But the Crusaders once again conquered the city in 1191; however, before they did so Saladin himself reduced the great seaport to rubble. The agony and pathos of this self-destruction were poignantly recorded in several Arabic sources. Here is the evidence of one writer; the quotation begins after the Crusaders have captured both Acre and Jaffa and are on their way to attack Ashkelon:

"[Saladin was] informed that [the Crusaders] were determined to rebuild Jaffa and strengthen it with soldiers and equipment. He, therefore, convened his advisers and consulted them about Ascalon: whether the right thing to do was to destroy it or not. They agreed upon its destruction for fear lest the enemy

Ruined ramparts *mark Ashkelon's ancient defensive line. The 1.2-mile-long wall was purposely destroyed by Saladin in 1191 to prevent Ashkelon from falling into the hands of the Crusaders. The Islamic defenders feared that with Ashkelon in Christian hands, the Crusaders could cut off the road to Jerusalem and then march on the Holy City.*

An anonymous Arab source poignantly described the scene: "The people entered the town crying and clamoring. Ascalon was a town likable to the heart, with firm walls and mighty structures, which people liked to inhabit. The people of the town were deeply saddened and wailed strongly because of the town's destruction, and because of their having to leave their homeland."

would reach it and occupy it, and by means of it he would occupy Jerusalem, and at the same time would cut off the road to Egypt. [As a result of that decision, Saladin] left his brother al-Malik al-'Adil [Abu Bakr] to face the enemy, and he himself went to destroy Ascalon on the dawn of Wednesday, the 18th of Sha'ban 387 [September 11, 1191].

"It was a very painful thing for him. He said: 'I would rather be bereaved of all my children than destroy a single stone of it. But if God foreordained anything, it is bound to be carried out.' He started destroying it on the dawn of Thursday, the 19th of Sha'ban [September 12, 1191]. He divided the wall [among the members of his army] and gave each commander and each group of the army a certain section and a certain tower to destroy.

"The people entered the town crying and clamoring. Ascalon was a town likable to the heart, with firm walls and mighty structures, which people liked to inhabit. The people of the town were deeply saddened and wailed strongly because of the town's destruction, and because of their having to leave their homeland . . . .

"The Sultan and his sons exerted themselves tremendously in ruining the town, with the purpose that the enemy would not get wind [of the operation], and rush to the town to prevent its destruction. The people [i.e., those who carried out the destruction] were at that night very hard and very exhausted because of what they had endured in the town's destruction.

"A person sent by al-Malik al-'Adil informed [the Sultan] that the Franks discussed with him terms of a settlement, by which the Muslims would have to cede certain lands [towns?]. The Sultan found advantage in it [in the proposed settlement agreement], for he knew how much the people were fed up with war and how heavy were their debts. He gave written permission to his brother to that effect, allowing him to conclude a settlement according to his lights.

"In the meantime destruction and the mobilization of people [for that purpose] went on, with the Sultan urging them to accelerate that operation. He also let them take whatever there had been in the royal granaries out of fear of the Frankish attack and the inability to move away their contents. He ordered the town set on fire, and fires were set in its houses. The town was an immense fortress. Destruction continued without stop until the last day of Sha'ban of that year [September 21, 1191]. When the destruction and burning were completed, the Sultan left Ascalon."[39]

We found considerable evidence of Saladin's 1191 destruction in many parts of Ashkelon. Near the Jerusalem Gate we found undermined and uprooted towers; the gold jewelry next to the Fatimid houses had been buried in destruction debris. On the beach and underwater, we found Roman columns and other debris that Saladin's men had used to fill in the medieval harbor, thus rendering it unusable for the Crusaders.

With the demolition of Ashkelon, Saladin initiated a policy of systematically destroying seaports all along the Mediterranean coast—seaports recaptured from the Crusaders. Never again would these seaports fall into Christian hands in usable condition should there be a renewal of the Crusades.

According to Professor David Ayalon, this Moslem policy—the destruction of their own ports for defensive purposes—was without parallel in recorded human history. It was a resounding admission of the naval hegemony of Christian Europe over that of Islam, which was established already by the 11th century A.D. without any great sea battle, and has not been seriously challenged since. This absolute victory on the sea reflected the steadily growing technological superiority of Christian Europe in general.

European naval dominance eventually changed the face of the globe. In searching for the safest and least expensive routes to India in the late 15th century, western Europeans avoided overland routes across vast tracts of Moslem territory. Instead, they sailed, for example, around the Cape of Good Hope. They also sought to reach India by sailing west. And this of course led, quite accidentally, to the discovery of America.

Thus the demolition of Ashkelon, when put in its proper historical perspective, becomes a crucial facet of international power politics, the effects of which continue to be felt to this day.

As director of the excavations at Ashkelon, I owe so much to so many: First and foremost, to Ms. Shelby White and Leon Levy, our benefactors, whose intellectual involvement and generous financial support have made this long-term, large-scale project possible; to the Israel Antiquities Authority, its director, Amir Drori, and former director, Avi Eitan, who have facilitated and expedited the research; to Professors Benjamin Mazar and Philip J. King for their wise counsel; to the citizens of Ashkelon and their mayor, the Honorable Eli Dayan, for their boundless hospitality; to the hundreds of volunteers for participating in the dig and field school; and to their teachers and supervisors, the professional staff, for bringing Ashkelon's heritage to light. In addition to staff already mentioned in the text and credits, I would like to thank several senior staff members for their contributions to this multidisciplinary effort: Douglas Esse (former associate director), Moshe ("Musa") Shimoni (majordomo), Larry and Dorothy Ingalls and Samuel Wolff (administrators and supervisors), Giora Solar and Benny Arubas (architects-draftsmen), Elizabeth Bloch-Smith, David Stacey, Ross Voss, Bill Griswold, Ron Tappy, Jonathan Elias (grid supervisors), Jane Waldbaum (supervisor and classical archaeologist), Charles Adelman and Joelle Cohen (ceramists), Barbara Hall and Valentine Talland (conservators), Ora Mazar (pottery restorer), Heather Campbell and Nicole Logan (registrars), Richard Saley (computer programmer), Ya'akov Meshorer and Haim Gitler (numismatists), Raphael Ventura (Egyptologist), Bill Grantham (zooarchaeologist), Mordechai Kislev (paleobotanist), Ya'akov Nir (hydrologist) and the late Hanan Lernau (paleoichthyologist). And finally, I want to express my indebtedness to Hershel Shanks, editor, and Steven Feldman, assistant editor, for their many contributions to this series on Ashkelon.

[1] Ya'akov Meshorer, *City Coins of Eretz-Israel and the Decapolis in the Roman Period* (Jerusalem: Israel Museum, 1985), p. 26.

[2] Shimon Applebaum, "Economic Life in Palestine," in *The Jewish People in the First Century*, ed. S. Safrai and M. Stern (Philadelphia: Fortress, 1976), vol. 2, p. 688 and n. 10, with reference to inscrip-

Endnotes continue on page 62

BEAUTY & UTILITY IN BONE
New Light on Bone Crafting

PAULA WAPNISH

*I*n Part II, Larry Stager described the unique dog cemetery discovered at Ashkelon in the Persian period.* Another unique aspect of the Persian period (538-332 B.C.) strata at the site is the quantity of worked animal bones—not only finished artifacts but also bones at various earlier stages in the manufacturing process, including unfinished pieces, rough-cut blanks and carving wastes.

Actually, worked bone and ivory artifacts have been found as early as the Middle Bronze Age II (1800-1550 B.C.) at Ashkelon. At other sites, such artifacts have been found from the Chalcolithic period (4000-3200 B.C.) and even earlier, so the 5th century B.C. *floruit* of the bone industry at Ashkelon was heir to a long tradition. Two later periods at Ashkelon also produced large quantities of bone from various stages in the manufacturing process—the Byzantine period (324-640 A.D.) and the Islamic period (640-1260 A.D.).

The quantity and variety of these worked bone finds at Ashkelon is unprecedented for a site in the eastern Mediterranean. From materials at Ashkelon, especially from the Persian period, we can now trace in considerable detail the traditions of bone working and even reconstruct the manufacturing process.

As a raw material, bone has several advantages: It is readily available, and it is strong, yet light and easy to work. Accordingly, it was a widely used raw material in antiquity. Combs, hair pins and cosmetic accessories were commonly fashioned from bone. Small implements such as needles, pins and fasteners or hinges were made entirely of bone, while metal tools such as knives were often fitted with bone handles. Boxes, chests, couches and other kinds of furniture were decorated with bone attachments or inlays. Bone was also used to make such things as dice, game counters, amulets and tokens (such as the one shown on p. 42).

The consistently high standard of workmanship of the bone products at Ashkelon testifies to the consummate skill and professional status of their makers. Some of the finer pieces, such as a handle in the form of a fluted column and some carved plaques, rise to the level of minor art.

Bone occurs in two forms. Cortical bone consists of

* Lawrence E. Stager, "Why Were Hundreds of Dogs Buried at Ashkelon?" page 20.

dense layers with no intervening spaces, except channels for small blood vessels. This type of bone forms the hard envelope surrounding the marrow. Cancellous bone, by contrast, is composed of tiny interwoven bony plates with a thin covering, giving it a porous structure and a soft texture. At the ends of long bones, cancellous bone provides points of attachment for sinews in the joints. Many bones, such as the radius (a bone in the lower fore limbs of mammals), are made up of both types of bone.

The dense structure of cortical bone is much more desirable for manufacturing purposes. In large decorative pieces, craftsmen took care that visible surfaces were not marred by unsightly sections of cancellous bone. Smaller pieces such as inlays required at least one side with no exposed porous surface (and a minimum of natural curvature). Bone used as handles for tools had to be sturdy enough to withstand the shock of repeated use. Overwhelmingly, the craftsmen at Ashkelon chose dense cortical bone over porous cancellous bone because of cortical bone's superior strength and smoothness.

Almost all of the bone used in the manufacturing process at Ashkelon comes from a few species of large domesticated animals: cattle (*Bos taurus*), camels (*Camelus sp.*, probably the dromedary) and donkeys (*Equus asinus*).

Only a few artifacts were fashioned from the bones of sheep (*Ovis aries*) or goats (*Capra hircus*). When sheep and goat bones were used, it was mostly for the manufacture of casual bone tools such as awls or points that were often made by the user, rather than by a large-scale professional manufacturer. Complete bones of sheep and goats, such as a metapodial, usually had to be employed because sheep and goat bones are too small to section into blanks.

No pig (*Sus scrofa*) bone was used even though pigs were very common in some periods and the males big enough to supply large bones. This may be due to the fact that many pig bones, such as those in the front and hind limbs, have much more torsion than bones of other domestic mammals. Most objects require straight sections of bone for which such pig bones are not suitable.[1]

Apparently cattle, camel and donkey bones were

Lace-like luxury. *Intricately patterned,
bone inlays, or mounts, carved in ajouré
(openwork) style, were often used to adorn
the edges of jewelry, or toiletry, boxes at
Ashkelon, where these pieces were found.
To create the pattern, the craftsman first
drilled a small hole and then used fine saws
and blades to enlarge it into decorative
shapes.*

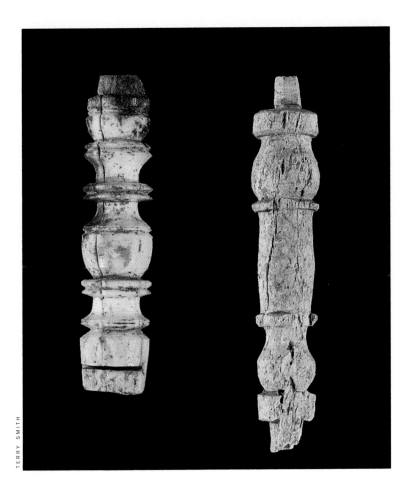

Not chess pieces. *These elegant, lathe-
made rods or spindles, the longest of which is
about 2.5 inches, were used to decorate
furniture and boxes. To create them, the
craftsman would attach a bone blank shaped
like a rod to a lathe-stock, which could then
be turned, thus rotating the bone about its
long axis. As the bone was rotated by one
worker, another would apply one of various
cutting tools to the rotating bone. The depth
and shape of the resulting cuts could be
controlled by the choice of tool and by the
angle and duration of application of the
blade. These pieces still possess the rough
ends that fit into the lathe-stock, possibly
indicating that they were rejects. The spindle
on the left was sawed longitudinally to
provide a flat side, unseen on its back, for
attachment to a flat surface.*

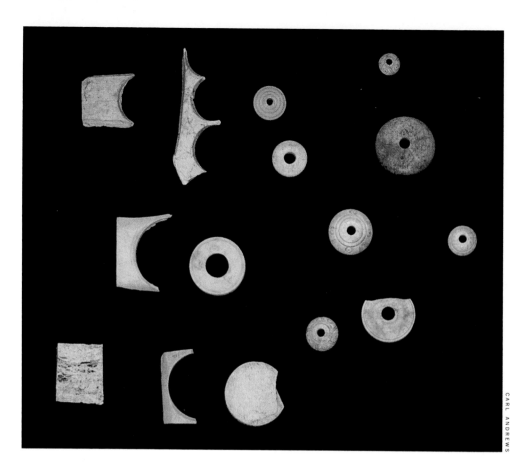

Three stages of carving. *This collection of pieces illustrates the latter two stages of the bone-carving process. The process began with the craftsman cutting a bone into workable segments (not shown). Next, a number of blanks were cut from the segments, in this case long bone shaft slices like the one in the lower left corner. Finally the craftsman, usually using a lathe, cut flat disks out of the blanks, leaving behind cut-off arcs like those seen at left. The disks could then be incised with designs for use as gaming pieces or drilled with holes to make buttons or whorls. The disk with a broken edge, at bottom right, is probably a reject. Some plano-convex buttons, or whorls, decorated with incised designs appear on the right.*

considered the most desirable, because they provided the greatest expanse of thick, relatively untwisted bone.

The high proportion of camel bone, however, is somewhat surprising. Domesticated camels are usually associated with desert nomadism rather than with settled urban life such as we find at Ashkelon. Yet camels must have been present in the city in sufficient numbers for their bones to have been regularly available to the bone carvers. The solution to the puzzle lies in the fact that Ashkelon served as both a crossroads and a terminus in the long distance trade in aromatics, such as incense, that originated in the Arabian peninsula.* Beginning in the Persian period, this trade was carried to a network of urban centers on Israel's southern coastal plain by camel caravans. The volume of shipments and the size of caravans greatly increased through time. Many of the camels that reached the city in these caravans must also have been sold, slain and eaten there. As a consequence, bone carvers had at their disposal an additional excellent source of desirable raw material.

Many bone artifacts unearthed at Ashkelon were found not in their primary contexts (that is, where they were originally used in antiquity) but in refuse dumps where they had accumulated after having been broken, lost or discarded. Nor is every stage of the manufacturing process equally well represented in the archaeological record. And as yet we have no clear evidence for the location of a bone workers' quarter or

* See Kjeld Nielsen, "Ancient Aromas, Good and Bad," *Bible Review*, June 1991.

bone tool *suq* (market) in the city. Despite these gaps in the data, however, the basic outline of the bone manufacturing process is clear.

At least three stages were involved in the progressive reduction of whole bones: first, they were reduced into large workable segments, then into more or less standard blanks from which artifacts could be fashioned, and finally into finished products.

In the initial stage as much as possible of the undesirable cancellous bone was removed while the maximum amount of dense cortical bone was retained.

The large segments of workable bone thus produced were then cut into manufacturing blanks. Depending on the size and shape of the original bone, it was possible at this intermediate stage to produce a variety of more or less standardized forms: flat sheets; square and round rods of varying thicknesses; round and half-round tubes and rods of different diameters.

In the final stage, these blanks were modified in different ways to produce different finished objects. Blanks of specific shape were selected in accord with the intended final product: thick or thin flat sheets for plaques, pieced inlays, disks, beads and tokens; large or small tubes or rods for handles or furniture fittings; long square strips or wedges for needles and pins. Several finished products could be made from a single kind of prepared blank. For example, flat sheets used to make disks could also be cut into thin square rods for needles and pins.

Each stage in the reduction process generated characteristic offcuts related in size and shape to the particular kind of blank or artifact being made. While the type and source species of the discarded offcuts and workable segments produced in the early stages of the reduction process can often be determined, the bone of finished artifacts is so much modified that it is difficult to tell from which part of what animal's skeleton the original raw material came. Fortunately, more than two-thirds of the bone artifacts from Ashkelon are unfinished, so it is possible in most cases to determine the source of the bone.

None of the bone carvers' tools have yet come to light. But careful examination of blanks and carving wastes as well as of finished pieces permits identification of many of the tools in the bone carvers' tool kit.

Each type of tool left behind distinctive marks, almost like fingerprints, on both artifacts and discarded wastes. While the exposed surfaces of finished objects were often smoothed to obliterate these marks, the underside of finished pieces and discarded waste retain traces of various tools used to work the bone.

The commonest tools were knives that could be used for shaving, scraping and smoothing as well as for carving. Delicate tasks such as slicing thin strips of bone from a prepared shaft could be accomplished with a double-handled draw knife. Numerous fine transverse parallel lines or "chatter marks" appear on bone smoothed by drawing a knife blade crosswise over the surface.

Initial shaping with coarse rasps and smooth finishing with fine files also left traces on the bone.

Various grades of saws, from fairly coarse to rather fine, were also employed, as is evident from tool marks on sawn sections of both artifacts and offcuts.

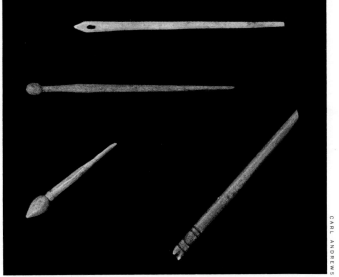

Pins and needles *for hair or cloth come in a variety of styles. The simple undecorated pins with ovoid heads, such as the second from the top, were cut by hand. All other types were made on a lathe.*

A center-bit scriber—a device with a cutting element set at a fixed radius from a center point—was almost certainly used to inscribe the "dot-and-ring" motif on the faces of dice. These designs are too perfectly symmetrical to have been incised freehand with a knife.

The lathe was certainly one of the most important tools used at Ashkelon. The early form of this tool was a modified bow drill, probably hand driven by the craftsman or an assistant. The piece to be worked was spun on this crude lathe. The regularity of the arcs the lathe produced is proof of its use. The telltale signs of these arced forms can be seen on completed objects and on waste pieces—on the end of solid rods and center indentations on flat surfaces where the worked piece had been fitted to the lathe stock. A diverse array of artifacts was produced on the lathe at Ashkelon: buttons and whorls, gaming pieces, decorative borders, finger rings, beads, hinges, pins and needles, furniture mounts, handles, small boxes and various circle-based decorative motifs.

The great quantity of worked bone excavated in Persian, Byzantine and early Islamic Ashkelon leaves little doubt about the enduring traditions of bone carving at the site. Even though new consumer fashions and evolving cultural mores may have dictated changes in finished products, underlying similarities in the shape of wastes, blanks and even some classes of artifacts over the span of a millennium and a half confirms the continuity of craft specialization. There are, after all, only so many ways to slice a bone in order to produce the required workable segments and manufacturing blanks (flat sheets, round, half-round and square rods) that formed the basis for the final products.

Interestingly, in the Hellenistic period (332-63 B.C.), Alexandria, Egypt, became the recognized leader in mass-produced bone carvings. What the situation was in the Persian period is difficult to tell. Perhaps Ashkelon was the leading center of that time.

Place your bets. *Less than half an inch wide, this finely wrought, cubical die exhibits the same arrangement of numbers on its faces as on a standard modern die. The exposed faces show a one, four and five; the unexposed faces bear a six opposite the one and a three and two opposite the four and five respectively. As in modern dice, the numbers consist of groups of dots, with each dot on this die surrounded by two concentric circles. The excellent symmetry of the circles strongly suggests that they were incised with a center-bit scriber, a tool that has a cutting element set at a fixed radius from a center point, similar to a compass.*

The endnote for this article appears on page 62.

Endnotes for Part III, (continued from p. 57)

tions nos. 1717-1724 and 2283 from Delos (in Launey and Roussel, *Inscriptions de Delos* [1937]).

[3] "Letter of Aristeas," line 115, in John R. Bartlett, *Jews in the Hellenistic World*, Cambridge Commentaries on Writings of the Jewish & Christian World 200 BC to AD 200 (Cambridge, UK: Cambridge Univ. Press, 1985), vol. I, part 1, p. 27.

[4] David Flusser, "Paganism in Palestine," in Safrai and Stern, *The Jewish People in the First Century* vol. 2, p. 1099.

[5] Applebaum, "Economic Life in Palestine," p. 688, n.10.

[6] On the authority of Julius Africanus (c. 170-243 A.D., cited in Eusebius, *Ecclesiastical History* Bk. I 6.2, 7.11). See *Eusebius, The History of the Church*, transl. G.A. Williamson (New York: Dorset, 1965), pp. 51, 55.

[7] Josephus, *The Jewish War* 1.21.42.

[8] Josephus, *Antiquities of the Jews* 17.11.5 (321).

[9] E.D. Hunt, *Holy Land Pilgrimage in the Later Roman Empire AD 312-460* (Oxford: Clarendon, 1984), p. 93 and n. 54, citing Origen, *Contra Celsum* 4.44 and Eusebius, *Onomasticon*, 168.

[10] Hunt, *Holy Land Pilgrimage*, p. 93, n. 55, citing Eustathius, *De Engastrimytho* 21 (ed. E. Klostermann, *Kleine Texte* 83 [1912]).

[11] This reconstruction of the evidence allows us to make sense of some other texts that mention the Wells of Abraham. Ibn Batutah observes that "you descend to these [Wells of Abraham] by broad steps leading to a chamber. On all four sides of the chamber are springs of water gushing out from the stone conduits." Antoninus Martyr, writing c. 560 A.D., describes the Well of Peace (*Puteus Pacis*) at Ashkelon in similar words: "There is a Well of Peace made after the manner of a theater, in which one descends by steps into the water." Garstang mistakenly located the Well of Peace in the apse of the large basilica, i.e., in his putative *bouleuterion*. Of course, when he completed the excavations in the apse, there was no well to be found. The Well of Peace is just another name for the Wells of Abraham or the Bir Ibrahim. And it is now clear that Origen, Antoninus Martyr and Ibn Batutah were describing all that remained of the Greco-Roman theater: "wells" noted for "their strange and extraordinary style of construction" and "built after the manner of a theater." Compare, for example, John Garstang, "The Fund's Excavation of Askalon," *Palestine Exploration Quarterly* (*PEQ*) 21 (1921), pp. 14-16; "The Excavations at Askelon," *PEQ* 22 (1922), pp. 112-117; "Askalon," *PEQ* 24 (1924), pp. 24-35.

[12] Cornelius Vermeule, "Askalon," in *M News* (Boston: Museum of the Fine Arts, 1991), pp. 85-89; Vermeule and Kristin Anderson, "Greek and Roman Sculpture in the Holy Land," in *Burlington Magazine*, 1981, pp. 7-20. Vermeule believes the sculpture excavated from the Severan basilica represents the "most splendid Roman imperial architectural sculpture to be found east of Ephesus and Corinth," p. 15.

[13] See Charles L. Meryon, *Travels of Lady Hester Stanhope, from the Completion of Her Memoirs, Narrated by Her Physician*, vol. 3 (1846), p. 162. From his drawing one can see the *Gorgoneion* in the center of the breastplate, with two griffins flanking some object below. A twin of the Ashkelon statue was recently excavated in Roman Beth-Shean—a larger-than-life-size marble statue (head missing) of a cuirassed soldier, probably an emperor, with the same motifs on the breastplate (for a photo, see **BAR**, July/August 1990, p. 24).

Unfortunately, Lady Hester Stanhope's basilica has been pillaged of all its masonry. However, Frank Koucky would locate it in an area that today is a parking lot for visitors to the beach, below the north slope of the south mound (al-Hadra) and just north of Grid 38 (lower). He could do this because of the detailed and accurate rendition of buildings and monuments of

Ashkelon published in 1855 by David Roberts (see p. 38), as viewed from a perspective on the north mound looking south.

[14] Professor Benjamin Mazar, personal communication.

[15] For an excellent discussion of the differences between Greco-Roman and Christian sexual codes and the ideal conduct during the second to fourth centuries A.D., see Robin Lane Fox, *Pagans and Christians* (New York: Knopf, 1987), especially chapter 7, aptly titled "Living Like Angels," pp. 336-374. Also see Paul Veyne, "Homosexuality in Ancient Rome," in *Western Sexuality: Practice and Precept in Past and Present Times*, ed. Philippe Ariès and André Béjin; transl. Anthony Forester (Oxford: Basil Blackwell, 1985), pp. 26-35.

[16] It is the same type of epithet as Astarte's *šem ba'al*, or "Name of Ba'al," attested at Ugarit in the Late Bronze Age and at Sidon in the fifth century B.C. These epithets represent a phenomenon in Canaanite, Phoenician and Israelite religion that Professor Frank Moore Cross characterizes as "hypostases of deity," in which aspects of transcendence become personified and activated in the cultic world (Cross, *Canaanite Myth and Hebrew Epic* [Cambridge, MA: Harvard Univ. Press, 1973], p. 30).

[17] Actually it is a series of doorways, each a bit smaller, reaching all the way to the inner sanctum, or holy of holies. The outermost doorway and facade (also the largest) is flanked by columns supporting a disc and crescent (symbol of either Tanit or Ba'al Ḥamōn) and a frieze of Egyptian uraei (cobras) above the lintel. One coin type reprinted here revealed the deity worshipped in the temple: on one side is a portrait of the beautiful Syrian empress Julia Domna; on the other is the goddess Tanit, as *panē Ba'al*, framed by the temple facade. See Meshorer, *City Coins of Eretz-Israel*, coins #47-50.

[18] See "Elagabalus," in *The Oxford Classical Dictionary*, ed. N.G.L. Hammond and H.H. Scullard (Oxford: Clarendon, 2nd ed., 1970), p. 377.

[19] For Ba'al Ḥamōn as "Lord of the Amanus," rather than the more common interpretation "Lord of the Brazier (or the Incense Altar)" (*Ba'al hamman*), see Cross, *Canaanite Myth and Hebrew Epic*, pp. 26-28, where he also links Ba'al Ḥamōn with a deity known in Hurrian as "El the One of the Mountain Ḥaman." To render Elagabal, "El of the Mountain," we derive -gabal from Arabic *jebel*, meaning "mountain," not from Hebrew or Punic *gbl*, meaning "boundary." It should be remembered that Emesa (*Homs*), Syria, the home of Elagabal, was established in the first century B.C. by Arabs, who identified strongly with Phoenician culture on the coast. See Anthony R. Birley, *Septimius Severus, the African Emperor* (New Haven, CT: Yale Univ. Press, rev. ed., 1988), pp. 68-71. For Empress Julia Domna's identification with (Dea) Caelestis, or Tanit, see Arnaldo Momigliano, *On Pagans, Jews, and Christians* (Middletown, CT: Wesleyan Univ. Press, 1987), p. 126.

[20] Personal communication from Professor Katherine Dunbabin.

[21] See John Boswell, *The Kindness of Strangers—The Abandonment of Children in Western Europe from Late Antiquity to the Renaissance* (New York: Pantheon, 1988). He is more sanguine than I am about the prospects of exposed infants and children being rescued.

[22] Naphtali Lewis, *Life in Egypt Under Roman Rule* (Oxford: Clarendon, 1985), p. 54.

[23] Michael Avi-Yonah, *The Holy Land: From the Persian to the Arab Conquest (536 B.C.-A.D. 640)* (Grand Rapids, MI: Baker Book House, 1977), pp. 195-196, and Applebaum, "Economic Life in Palestine," p. 648.

[24] Strabo, 16.2.29; Pliny, *Natural History* 19.32.101-107.

[25] John A. Riley, "The Pottery from the First Session of Excavation in the Caesarea Hippodrome," *Bulletin of the American Schools of Oriental Reasearch* 218 (1975), p. 30, n. 20

[26] Riley, "The Pottery from the First Session,"

p. 30.

[27] Ann Killebrew of the Hebrew University has added another type of amphora (her Type A found at Deir el-Balah) to the repertoire of so-called Gaza wine jars. Our results at Ashkelon confirm her suggestion.

[28] Mitchell Allen, "The Ashkelon Regional Archaeological Survey." Paper presented at the national AIA convention in San Francisco, December, 1990. This research will soon appear as part of his Ph.D. dissertation being completed at the Institute of Archaeology, UCLA.

[29] See Ann Killebrew's chapter on Roman and Byzantine pottery, final report of the excavations at Deir el-Balah (forthcoming).

[30] Gabi Mazor, "Wine Presses in the Negev," *Qadmoniot* (1981), pp. 51-60.

[31] Hunt, *Holy Land Pilgrimage*, p. 99.

[32] Philip Mayerson, "The Pilgrim Routes to Mount Sinai and the Armenians," *Israel Exploration Journal* 32 (1982), pp. 44-57; for Ararat, see Eusebius' *Onomasticon* 2-4, ed. E. Klostermann, *Die griechischen christlichen Schriftstellar der ersten drei Jahrhunderte* (Leipzig 1904, reprinted 1966).

[33] Hunt, *Holy Land Pilgrimage*, pp. 130-131.

[34] Riley, "The Pottery from the First Session," p. 30, n. 20.

[35] Myriam Rosen-Ayalon, "The Islamic Jewellery from Ashkelon," in *Jewellery and Goldsmithing in the Islamic World*, An International Symposium, Jerusalem, ed. Na'ama Brosh (Jerusalem: Israel Museum, 1991), pp. 9-20.

[36] These Fatimid fortifications are usually attributed incorrectly to the Crusader Period.

[37] William of Tyre, *A History of Deeds Done Beyond the Sea*, transl. E.A. Babcock and A.C. Krey (New York: Columbia Univ. Press, 1943), pp. 17, 22. For a very readable account of Ashkelon in the Crusader period, see Meron Benvenisti, *The Crusaders in the Holy Land* (Jerusalem: Israel Universities Press), pp. 114-130.

[38] We know this because of the five churches at Ashkelon during the time of the Crusaders, four were Latin and one was Byzantine (Greek), namely, Santa Maria Viridis. Before our excavations scholars usually thought this church was located next to the sea (in Grid 50), near a Muslim saint's tomb known as Maqam al-Hadra, or Shrine of the Green (Lady), from which the south mound took its name. We now know that the church was located on the opposite side of the city.

[39] Translated from the Arabic by Professor David Ayalon of Hebrew University.

[40] David Ayalon, "The Mamluks and Naval Power—a Phase of the Struggle between Islam and Christian Europe," *Proceedings of the Israel Academy of Sciences and Humanities*, vol. 1 (Jerusalem, 1965), pp. 1-12. Also "Islam versus Christian Europe: the Case of the Holy Land," in *Pillars of Smoke and Fire: the Holy Land in History and Thought*, ed. Moshe Sharon (Johannesburg, 1988), pp. 247-256.

Endnote for "Bone Crafting," p. 58

[1] Except for antler, there is no worked wild animal bone, though unworked bone of hartebeast (*Alcelaphus* sp.), a large African antelope, have been recovered at the site. This is not suprising, since the manufacturing process needed a constant and reliable source of raw material that hunting could not supply. About 20 small sections of sawn antler indicate that it too was used as a raw material at Ashkelon, but so far no objects in antler have been found, nor have any bones of the Persian fallow deer (*Dama mesopotamica*) from which it came. The antler was probably obtained through trade since the fallow deer is not a regular inhabitant of the southern coastal plain. Antler is much stronger than bone and thus preferred for handles and other items that need to withstand hard use. The very small amount of worked antler compared to bone is probably due to its greater cost as an import, which outweighed its greater desirability as a raw material.

Readers Vote to Print Erotic Oil Lamps

The results are in. Our readers voted overwhelmingly to print pictures of the erotic, indeed pornographic, oil lamps excavated at Ashkelon.

Here is the count:

1. Don't print the pictures 20%
(138 votes)

2. Print the pictures 50%
(351 votes)

3. Print them, but with a perforation allowing them to be removed 30%
(214 votes)

Combining the second and third categories, both of which voted to print the pictures in one way or another, the vote was 80 percent to 20 percent.

Nevertheless, to accommodate the sensitivities of those who regard these pictures as inappropriate or who fear they might fall into the hands of children, we have printed them in such a way that they can easily be cut out without damaging the magazine or removing any other editorial matter.

Many readers accompanied their votes with comments. We print a representative sample below.

Don't Print Them

I think most (right-minded) people will agree that the human form, whether draped or otherwise, cannot be obscene. On the other hand, the depiction of explicit sexual acts, even on archaeological discoveries, in a semipopular magazine such as **BAR** (as distinguished from a scholarly dissertation) raises a different set of questions. What purpose will pictures of the erotic lamps serve in this case? Will they help substantiate the dating of the dig or contribute significantly to our understanding of the underlying culture? Or will they only satisfy a kind of "Gee, whiz" curiosity? If there is a *substantial* reason for printing the pictures (other than proving that the ancients enjoyed a variety of sexual positions), then go ahead; otherwise, there would be no point in unnecessarily offending many of your readers. Verbal description should suffice.
David H. Fax
Pittsburgh, Pennsylvania

This is a tough call. I thoroughly support the free exchange of thought that takes place in **BAR**. Obviously, the activities portrayed on the lamps were a part of life in that period—thank goodness, or we wouldn't be having this discussion. I must assume that most of the readers of **BAR** already "know about it." That leaves only the "visual impact" argument and that is strong; but, after consideration, I come down on the

side of propriety.
Edgar O. Fox
Tipton, Oklahoma

I vote against. But all my kids voted for.
Julie Markham
Houston, Texas

I have no problem with the naked human form, but I feel that depiction of that form involved in a sex act crosses the line into pornography. The age of the material does not render it nonpornographic.
Penny Lovestedt
Renton, Washington

My mind is a precious gift from God. I don't want such dirt dumped on me.
Mrs. James D. Poole
Columbia, South Carolina

My 14-year-old daughter enjoys your magazine and we just renewed our subscription. I would hate to have to edit a Biblical book that comes into my home for this kind of obscenity.
Dennis R. Cavender
Warfordsburg, Pennsylvania

The inspired apostle Paul wrote in Philippians 4:8: "Finally, brethren, whatever is true, whatever is honorable, whatever is right, whatever is pure, whatever is lovely, whatever is of good repute, if there is any excellence and if anything worthy of praise, let your mind dwell on these things." I do not see the publication of photos of erotic lamps fulfilling this Biblical admonition.
Roger K. Myers, Pastor
Grace Brethren Church
Waynesboro, Pennsylvania

Genesis 3:7 reads, "And the eyes of them both were opened, and they knew that they were naked; and they sewed fig leaves together, and made themselves aprons." There are numerous lessons to be learned from this verse, but one is the lesson of decency. Note that Adam and Eve were the only humans present when they had opened eyes. Their shame evidently was for how they appeared before a Holy and Righteous God. Since that time those who consider how they appear before God have sought to "abstain from all appearance of evil" (1 Thessalonians 5:22). Therefore, the question should be: "Which of your readers believe the erotic lamps of Ashkelon will give honor and glory to God?"
Permit me to close with His words. "Have no fellowship with the unfruitful works of darkness, but rather reprove them. For it is

a shame even to speak of those things which are done of them in secret. But all things that are reproved are made manifest by the light: for whatsoever doth make manifest is light" (Ephesians 5:11-13).
Malcolm D. Redman, Jr., Pastor
Bethany Baptist Church
Ft. Lauderdale, Florida

Print Them

Print the pictures of the lamps. This is life as it was. If someone is worrying about their children seeing it, clip it out.

I do not want anyone deciding what I may see or not see. I'm not a child. I'm almost 69. I'm a big girl now, in more ways than one, and I do not appreciate anyone restricting my knowing (or seeing) or hearing the truth.

I raised seven children and if they asked, they were told; they are all religious and good family people. Knowing the truth won't hurt, but hiding it will.
Evelyn B. Meyer
McMinnville, Oregon

Don't underestimate children's knowledge of sex.

Don't underestimate the value of the added excitement of sex in interesting a child in *any* subject, including archaeology.
David Lipman
Spring Valley, New York

Keep us as fully informed on the past as you possibly can, whether or not what you find is offensive to some people's professed sensibilities. The past contained good and evil, just as does the present—and denial doesn't change it one bit.
June R. Rothlauf
Burlington, Iowa

Don't reduce **BAR** to the level of a children's magazine.
Maxine Rapley
Toronto, Ontario
Canada

Why so much fear and trepidation? What are you afraid of? And why ask *us*? Editor, make up your *own* mind, and then stand up for what you believe.

The would-be censors of morality love this sort of waffling.
Chris Nelson
Rockford, Illinois

I can't believe after all the scholastic griping you do concerning the lack of publication of the Dead Sea Scrolls you would even think about withholding information!

Jeanette McKinney-Heifner, Graduate
Student
Department of Near Eastern Studies
University of California, Berkeley
Berkeley, California

I'm a pastor of a Southern Baptist church.
I want photos for clear information!

Jim Meek
Reno, Nevada

About a year ago some local high school
kids came around selling magazine subscrip-
tions as a school band uniform fundraiser.
My only previous exposure to **BAR** was an
occasional brief look in the doctor's or
dentist's office. Anyway, the kids didn't have
much on their list to choose from so I signed
up for an introductory subscription to **BAR**.
And you know, it was one of the smartest
things I have ever done. Some of the articles are positively riveting.

I am neither student nor scholar, but more
of an innocent bystander who enjoys **BAR**
about as much as my first love, aviation
and flying. Maybe I don't even belong in
the fraternity of **BAR** subscribers, because I
take a less-than-scholarly approach to it all.
That is not to say that I feel that detail and
accuracy are unimportant in the reports on
the digs and the ancients, only that it in-
terests me less than the articles' summary
and overall impression. Actually, I enjoy
the lively section of Queries & Comments
because that's where the readers' expressions
can be heard by all.

Should **BAR** print the pictures of the
erotic lamps? Absolutely! That was a part
of life. After all, sex was created by God. It
was made dirty by the mind of man. And I
suspect that men, and women for that matter, are not so different today than they
were 2,000 years ago. You may catch a little
flak on the pictures from a few closed minds
but that triviality will be more than com-
pensated for by the service to education
you will thereby provide your subscribers.
So print it all, for all of us. You won't shock
anybody. In fact, it would be a serious disservice to withhold it.

Mike Day
Delano, Minnesota

I object to the sadistic violence depicted in
many archaeological finds, but I do not think
that is a reason to suppress their display.

Rev. Winsome Munro
Assistant Professor
St. Olaf College
Northfield, Minnesota

If we see depictions of war, pillage and plun-
der, why not sex?

D. Kahn
Cambria, California

Ancient child sacrifice is much more rep-
rehensible than erotic lamps—at least to
me. I can't recall anyone objecting to the
report of that (Lawrence E. Stager and
Samuel R. Wolff, "Child Sacrifice at
Carthage—Religious Rite or Population
Control?" Jan./Feb. 1984).

Morris Stern
Plainview, New York

I know of only one person in history who
was conceived without the process of sex;
and that is more theology than biology. If
you withhold publication of an archaeological find because you are afraid some Sunday school teacher might be momentarily
embarrassed, then you have surrendered your
ethical position as an impartial arbiter in
the dissemination of Biblical archaeological
information.

David F. DeLoera
Calumet City, Illinois

Print them! By appealing to the prurient
interest, your readership will increase ten-
fold. Works every time.

Patricia Michl
Sumner, Washington

The goal of archaeology is information, not
judgment. Truth and knowledge are not
served through censorship. Archaeology is
the study of *all* human history, not just the
lives of the saints.

Paul and Alice Weis
Spokane, Washington

People should be looking at such things as
history and keep their minds out of the
gutter.

Phyllis A. Hanscom
Gold Hill, Oregon

Understanding how perverse Ashkelon had
become before God's condemnation is valuable toward gaining a full appreciation of
Scripture. The self-evident truth of photos
eliminates imaginative conjectures and es-
tablishes a solid basis for understanding.

Paul A. Zellmer
Fontana, California

Like the apostle Paul, "I know and am
persuaded in the Lord Jesus that nothing is
unclean in itself; but it is unclean for anyone who thinks it is unclean" (Romans
14:14).

Arch B. Taylor, Jr.
Clinton, South Carolina

"Ye shall know the truth, and the truth
shall make you free" (John 8:32).

Charles A. Logan
Redmond, Oregon

Your magazine is excellent. You good people
know it is excellent. Most of the people
reading it know that it is excellent. Why
bother with a vote relating to any subject.
You'll never please everyone.

C. W. Granrath
San Antonio, Texas

Print Them With a Perforation, Facilitating Removal

As a mother, and as a person concerned
with the deteriorating morals of this society, I would say no to printing photos of
the erotic oil lamps. However, as a person
with a B.A. in historic preservation, and as
someone whose dream is to be a Biblical
archaeologist, I feel that they should be
published. One of **BAR**'s goals is the dissemination of current archaeological research, and you would be doing your readers a disservice not to publish. My vote
therefore is for a perforated page so that
those with children, or Sunday schools, etc.
can remove them at will.

The Greeks were right that the human
form is beautiful, but there is a time and a
place to show it. Despite the erotic oil lamps
probably being pornographic, I feel that
BAR is such a time and a place. I am glad
the editors care enough for the sensitivities
of their readers to ask for their opinion.
We need more such responsible persons in
our too-often sex- and violence-oriented
media.

Janet Bhagat
Hampton, New Hampshire

In the interest of getting your wonderful
magazine into schools and libraries, I vote
to have a removable section for the erotic
lamps.

Patty Curran
Cambridge, Massachusetts

I use past editions of **BAR** in my waiting
room for my congregation to read should
they arrive early for an appointment.

Thank you for being gracious and ethical enough to poll your constituents to see
how they feel. Everyone will not be satis-
fied with the outcome; however, we all can
rejoice in the Christian spirit of cooperation that is being exercised.

Theron T. Stuart, Pastor
Faith Baptist Church and Easley
Christian School
Easley, South Carolina

I vote for the perforations. But don't make
the perforations too well, lest my copy come
with those pages missing.

Jonah Wahrman
Allentown, Pennsylvania